IN

THE

BEGINNING,

GOD . . .

A Glimpse.
It's just a Glimpse.

The beginning of the world and the fall of man.
Everything is in the beginning; according to the Bible. (fp)

MIN. FRANZO PAMPHILE

authorHOUSE®

AuthorHouse™
1663 Liberty Drive
Bloomington, IN 47403
www.authorhouse.com
Phone: 1 (800) 839-8640

Published by AuthorHouse 02/19/2019

ISBN: 978-1-7283-0094-8 (sc)
ISBN: 978-1-7283-0098-6 (e)

Print information available on the last page.

This book is printed on acid-free paper.

To the Lord GOD Almighty be the glory, dominion and power, forever and ever. To our Lord and Savior JESUS CHRIST be power, riches, wisdom, might, honor, glory, blessing and dominion forever and ever. His blood cleanses us from all sin. Amen!

Less of me Lord, less of me Oh Lord; More of you, Lord. Yes. More of You, forever and ever. Amen! Glory be to our GOD.

Ephesians 3:20,21 "Now to Him who is able to do far more abundantly beyond all that we ask or think, according to the power that works within us, to Him be the glory in the church and in Christ Jesus to all generations, forever and ever. Amen."

Before anything else that will follow, we would like to remind the reader of two things: this book is neither a Bible commentary, an encyclopedia, a bible reference, nor a bible dictionary; this book is just presenting a glimpse of the Glory of GOD in the beginning.

As I understand it... By the help of the Holy Spirit, within the boundaries of my limitation, but by the authority of the Holy Scriptures, that the most High allows me to access. In John16:12, the Lord said to the disciples: "I still have many things to say to you, but you cannot bear them now".

One does not really have to agree with some of the things which are written in this book, however it will illuminate and bring a little understanding to those who are seeking for the truth; the truth that will make you consider a question that some ask, and have doubt to know if GOD does really exist? We will answer this daring question in a moment. Meanwhile... EVERYTHING IS IN THE BEGINNING. THE BEGINNING OF THE WORLD IS GREAT AND PERFECT. GOD HAD A SPECIFIC PLAN FOR MANKIND, BUT SIN AND DEATH GOT MIXED INTO IT. DID GOD MAKE A MISTAKE? DID HE MISS SOMETHING? CAN WE SAY SO? NO. GOD DID NOT MAKE A MISTAKE. Well, on the sixth day in Genesis 1:31 said: "GOD saw everything that HE had made, and indeed, it was very good"...

I am very thankful to so many people that some might say that this book is not really about the beginning of the world. The most important of it all for me is the message that the Bible brings to us. It's fascinating, filled with truths and wonders, filled with just a glimpse of the glory of GOD; let me repeat that: "filled with just a glimpse of the glory of GOD". The Bible contains a message that needs to be shared and told. Yes, indeed. This message is worthy to be shared. Why is it worth sharing? What does it mean to me? We all were born at a certain moment in life, we grew up, we have accomplished a few things, we got old and we die. Is that the routine? Well, indeed it seems to be. Was it designed that way? I personally don't think it was. However, what can we say? According to the Bible many didn't have the privilege to get old. Some have passed away a young age, middle age, pre-old age, old age and even premature age. What's going on? What happened? What's happening?

There's a book that describes life and where one can or will find it. John 1:4 said: "in Him was life, and the life was the light of men" (KJV). Further down in the 14th chapter of the same book of John, at verse 6, Jesus' response unto Thomas for the disciples about their inquiry for not knowing where He is going, and that they do not know the way, said: "I am the Way, the Truth, and the Life; no man cometh unto the Father, but by me" (KJV). WOW! Martha, one of Lazarus' sisters, came to meet the Lord after her brother had been buried for four (4) days. She got into a conversation with the Lord in John 11:17-25. The conversation got very serious..., but the Lord confirmed to Martha these words: "I am the resurrection and the life..."

Mankind has been looking for a kind of piety, so that others can see their goodness or, that they can show they are good. In the gospel according to Luke, it is said at chapter 18 in verses 18 and 19: "A ruler questioned Him, saying, Good Teacher, what shall I do to inherit eternal life?" (v19) And Jesus said to him, "Why do you call me good? No one is good except GOD alone" (NASB). The Bible has painted over and over again the fall of mankind and the solution provided for his redemption, but mankind had made a choice, but GOD... Hallelujah!!! In his goodness (in His love for us, this great unconditional love), since He knew and knows the outcome of man's choice, yes indeed, He knows of man's decision, (good GOD Almighty! A friend of mind always said), provided an escape goat, had a master plan, let me repeat: "the Lord had a master plan", (Genesis 3:21) right there in the beginning, brought hope for mankind; because only GOD can go around His word. I repeat only GOD can go around His word. The Bible declares in Romans 3:23 "for all have sinned and fall short of the glory of GOD." In Psalms 14:3 it is also written: "all have turned away, all have become corrupt; there is no one who does good, not even one." And there are a bunch of other references in the Bible that will get you very depressed and make you very sad, if you are the type who can accept the truth, you will see that it is true; look in Psalm 53:3, Jeremiah 5:1. But the Lord Jesus has declared in John 8:12 "I am the Light of the world; he who follows Me will not walk in the darkness, but will have the light of life". It also describes death. It describes it by choice and disobedience; Genesis 2:17 said: "but from the tree of the knowledge of good and evil you shall not eat, for in the day that you eat from it you will surely die". You can clearly see that The Lord GOD is not a dictator. Right there in the garden, as HE finished creating man like HIM, (Gen 1:26,27), after the likeness of the Word and HIM, He is not indeed a dictator. Death is in the beginning for training, knowledge, obedience and for consequence; and since man yields to it, the outcome has become very obvious. Sin was not in eating the fruit of the tree. Sin started in the heart of man by yielding to the voice of the serpent, instead of staying steadfast on the commandment of GOD. Sin was in disobeying what the Lord GOD has commanded; because man was supposed to continue in the process that GOD has set for him to follow. "For the wages of sin is death" according to Romans 6:23. Death is the opposite of life. Death is cessation of life. In the book of Sirach 15:17 it is said: "Before each person are life and death, and whichever one chooses will be given". Adam had perfect knowledge; if it weren't so, GOD would not inculcate these rules to him. So, Adam knew very well, what the Lord GOD said. Adam made a choice and that choice has caused a lot of chaos. We will discuss that in the third book in Genesis chapter 3. There are nine things of the Bible that get me into deep thinking, that make some sense to me, and that are also very dear to me:

1- Why some believe that there is a GOD, and why some don't?

2- Where did GOD find coats of skins (Gen 3:21 KJV) to dress Adam and Eve up?

3- How would a Savior be born of a virgin who knew no man?

4- Why did GOD send His only begotten Son to save a perishing world that HE had cursed?

5- Why Jesus gave a bunch of teachings and a chain of parables in the gospel of Luke from chapter 10 thru 16, but in one particular chapter which is chapter 16, verses 19-31, He painted a stunning indisputable reality of **what happened when someone dies.**

6- Why would the disciples ask Him about the sign of His coming (Matthew 24:3) and the end of the age?

7- Why was Jesus hated so much?

8- Why Jesus was arrested, tortured, died and resurrected?

9- Exodus 32, 33 and 34. Yes, chapters 32, 33 and 34 of the book of Exodus. Read them over and over again. **<u>The Lord is not a dictator</u>**.

So, what did you see especially in Exodus 34? What did you comprehend?

Proverbs 4:1-7 said:

1 "Hear, O ye children, the instruction of a father, and give ear to learn understanding.

2 For I do give you a good doctrine: therefore forsake ye not my law.

3 For I was my father's son, tender and dear in the sight of my mother,

4 When he taught me, and said unto me, let thine heart hold fast my words: keep my commandments, and thou shalt live.

5 Get wisdom: get understanding: forget not, neither decline from the words of my mouth.

6 Forsake her not, and she shall keep thee: love her and she shall preserve thee.

7 Wisdom is the beginning: get wisdom therefore: and above all thy possession get understanding". 1599 Geneva Bible (GNV)

Proverbs 4:1-7

1 "Hear, my sons, the instruction of a father, and pay attention in order to gain and to know intelligent

discernment, comprehension, and interpretation [of spiritual matters].

2   For I give you good doctrine [what is to be received]; do not forsake my teaching.

3   When I [Solomon] was a son with my father [David], tender and the only son in the sight of my mother [Bathsheba],

4   He taught me and said to me, Let your heart hold fast my words; keep my commandments and live.

5   Get skillful and godly Wisdom, get understanding (discernment, comprehension, and interpretation); do not forget and do not turn back from the words of my mouth.

6   Forsake not [Wisdom], and she will keep, defend, and protect you; love her, and she will guard you.

7   The beginning of Wisdom is: get Wisdom (skillful and godly Wisdom)! [For skillful and godly Wisdom is the principal thing.] And with all you have gotten, get understanding (discernment, comprehension, and interpretation)".

Amplified Bible, Classic Edition (AMPC)

Would anyone understand the love of GOD? But here's that same question: "Does GOD exist"? Here is the answer. Get ready. It's not that simple. It requires some thinking, reading and meditation:

1- Genesis 1:1 "In the beginning, GOD created the heaven and the earth. (Rev. A. R. Bernard, after quoting those words, said: "That's where faith begins". John 1:1-5. please read this portion at least 3 times.

2- Genesis 1:26 "And GOD said, Let us make man (humankind) in our image, according to our likeness, (some other version say: "after our likeness: and let them have dominion"... Gen 1:26 And GOD said "Let us make man in our image"... So, GOD created man according to His likeness and resemblance. GOD created another God...

3- Isaiah saw the throne of the Lord (Isa 6:1-7 or read the whole chapter) Ezechiel saw visions of GOD. Read Ezekiel 1: 1-28, please read the whole chapter 1.

4- John saw His throne, Rev 4. etc...

5- David in one of his meditation, perhaps Psalms 19:1 "The heavens are telling the glory of GOD; and their expanse is declaring the work of His hands."

Remember that this book is only a glimpse. Yes, just a glimpse... It is written to bring honor, glory to the word of GOD, and celebrate salvation that is only possible through one man, JESUS the Christ, the Son of the living GOD.

This is indeed a perfect example that shows the existence of GOD; that HE created man on earth with the dust of the earth, but in his image and likeness/ Does that mean that He already knew that He was going to die for His creation? Wait a minute now! Genesis 2:18-20, emotions. Emotions? Yes, emotions. Read it again. Yes, why not seeing "emotions"? Because here, The Lord is spending time with Adam; HE had already seen, felt, and comprehended the loneliness of Adam. (Adam is not too happy, he is sad, he is missing something and the Lord sees it). HE decided to take care of that by making a helper for him to make him complete. (the following is my paraphrase, my assumption; not in the Bible) I am the Lord. I made you. I am looking after you. I am leading and taking you somewhere..., but Adam was listening, or maybe was in awe, still absorbing information, maybe daydreaming, or trying to process and bear so much information. The guy is in the garden of Eden, a garden planted by GOD. Things must have been so beautiful, peaceful and so wonderful in there that he was in silent and contemplation. Would you stay focus and follow my instructions? Would you be patient and enjoyed what I have already set in front of you. I have made all these things to make you understand and see that I have a plan I am going by, I placed you here to come and enjoy the ride with me. I have already given the rules to you. Let us go! But...??? Finally, it's like the Lord is catering to us but at the same time, He is stern and firm in his rules and principles.

There are plenty of other important teachings in the Bible. Will you check them out? It is written in John 6:63 "It is the spirit who gives life; the flesh profits nothing; the words that I have spoken to you are spirit and are life". When someone discover something that is good, will he or she keep it selfishly for their well-being or try to make a profit of it or live off it? Jesus gave a few short parables to the believers so that they could accept or reject, go tell about Him, tell what is to come, and also that they could cherish for themselves, whether one believes it or not, the Bible is a book that is worth reading. Other people have often described how it has been helping them succeed in their enterprise. The list of thanks that follows constitute a group of personal acquaintances and friends whom, have been a great support in the realization of that book project.

ACKOWLEDGEMENTS
AND THANKS

To my late mother Marie Iphonise E Pamphile, a strong praying servant of the Lord, who never stopped praying for me, and she remained strong in the faith until she went in the presence of the Lord on Dec 24th, 2013. And to my dad Cemezier Pamphile who is with the Lord.

To Jackie Posey, when I witnessed to her, told me that there was something else that I should have been doing, and she diligently started looking for the right Bible school for me until she found the right one.

To my uncle, the Reverend Jean Montira Edmond and his lovely wife, a great man of God from whom, I heard and learned a great prayer of faith, that got me thinking about; What is it that is impossible for GOD to do?

To Barry Borror and Antonio Bourciquot who stood firm in their conviction of standing out for me, in a time when everything was falling apart around me, and whom GOD used, to get me in the great United States of America.

To Julienne Estera Pamphile, the mother of my son Nathan, to whom I cannot find words to describe my gratitude and thanks.

To Dr. Darryl Claybon, a great man of God, a thinker, a great teacher and a scholar at (ITC Interdenominational Theological Center) who taught me how to read and approach the Bible; And he added that saying: ***when the student is ready, the teacher will appear.***

To Ms. Susie Caswell, a very kind and sweet woman of God, with a great and extraordinary understanding, at ITC.

To Dr. Gerald Durley, a great mentor, and his sweet wife who have allowed me in their circle.

To Veronica Kulon, a friend with a great command of the language, whom has given her precious time in making this book understandable.

To another very good friend Ken Atli, and his lovely wife Stephanie Atli who have contributed greatly in the realization of this project. They are friends you can count on in troubled times.

To Pastor Houseworth and Evangelist Bailey, two great men of GOD. They are Bible scholars and teachers. To two other great Pastors, (One in Union City and one in New York) whom from their teachings through the radio waves, I have learned a lot.

To Frantz Andre Altidor, Latosha Griffin, Francois Whitny, Hadiya Leger, Florence Ebwe, to Sammy and Dorothy Ngalame, Scotty, Greg Redmond, Elvis Cleavon, and George Lane, very great friends whom I cannot find words to express the understanding of friendship.

To all of you readers who will venture in reading this book. It is also dedicated to you. It will make you see and have another type of understanding about the word of GOD, the Bible; it may challenge some of your belief. But after all and above all, there's one GOD, one Lord, one Savior, and one King in whom, everything is.

INTRODUCING THE **"GLIMPSE Series"**, *bringing honor and glory to GOD alone and to HIS Word. The Bible alone explains the Bible. And the Spirit of GOD will help you understand His Word once you open that book.*

What is "The GLIMPSE Series"?

"The Glimpse Series" is a project that will study, opine, blog and present excerpts, essays, booklets on words, verses, passages and books of the Bible. The project came in mind when considering the goodness of GOD (Spirit), we were able to see GOD like king David (Psalms). Psalm 142:7 "Set me free from my prison, that I may praise your name. Then the righteous will gather about me because of your goodness to me."

The book you are about to read is very intense with Bible references and will bounce you vigorously from time to time into reading and checking them out. The title "IN THE BEGINNING, GOD..." is the first in a series of 3 books that are coming out very soon under the *"GLIMPSE Series,"* which will study, and opine on the first three chapters of the book of Genesis, and on different books, chapters, passages, verses and words of the Bible such as: Grace, Blood, Love, Mercy, With (and lo I am with you always...), Peace, Humility, Hell, Darkness, Kingdom, Heaven, King, Servant, Eternity, Law, Resurrection, Baptism, Precepts, Ordinances, understanding. It will also study sentences, paragraphs, sections, etc... The "Glimpse Series" will bring short writings, essays and booklets on a variety of important subjects of the Holy Book. The first book is about Genesis chapter 1. Remember what is written on the cover of this book. it's just a glimpse. The second book is about Genesis chapter 2. And the third will be about Genesis chapter 3.

MOTIVATION

How can you know of GOD and about the Bible if you don't read the Bible? How can you know GOD if you do not read the book that reveals GOD to you? How are you claiming you are a Christian and in the Lord and you don't want to show yourself approved to GOD as a workman...? In the (NJB) version it is written like this: 2 Tim 2:15 said: "Make every effort to present yourself before GOD as a proven worker who has no need to be ashamed, but who keeps the message of the truth on a straight path"; and 1 Peter 3:15 also said: "Simply proclaim the Lord Christ holy in your hearts and always have your answer ready for people who ask you the reason for the hope that you have." **The whole purpose behind this project is to get its readers (Christians or non-Christians, religious or non-religious) to not only,** *to read the Bible,* **but to go deeper by studying it.** In his book "All about the Bible", Sidney Collett starts his first chapter like this: "A world without a Bible". We are not in his mind to know what he meant or means, but he has a point. I would even add "a world without a guide".

Another purpose for this booklet, is to show that ***the Bible explains the Bible*** in a great major part of it; although that certain things maybe obscure for some but, if one really wants to seek GOD, know the Bible, or know about the Bible, he or she will be satisfied in their quest; Matthew 7:7-8 "Ask, and it will be given to you; Seek and you will find; Knock, and it will be opened to you. For everyone who asks receives, and he who seeks finds, and to him who knocks it will be opened." So with these words of Christ Jesus, the Holy Spirit will do the rest. There is enough in the Bible to satisfy the quest of knowing for everyone. Why reading the Bible? There are many other reasons I can think of but, here are a few: It is the only book that narrates the history of the world, it shows and describes a beginning and an end, where that time will come for everything to be new again. Actually, things have become new. You probably think of heresy when I said that. Indeed, things have become new again. Here are a few evidences:

1   I can go back all the way to Gen 3:21, GOD did not destroyed Adam and Eve, but HE had to abide by His commandment and decree. GOD had to obey to His own word.

2   GOD could have been done with us and started over another way, but HE found a way to go around what HE said.

3   Gen 4:1-2: Eve bore two sons. You all know about Cain and Abel. Notice that Eve acknowledged the goodness of GOD: "I have produced a man with the help of the Lord", said Eve at verse 1.

4   God has continued to be there, even going after Cain, to preach to him to acknowledge what he did and to repent; which Cain refused to do. (GOD is not a dictator)

5   GOD giving man instructions or crucial directives (Gen 2:15-17)

6   HE sent His son. No, let me say it this way: HE came to dwell among men for about 33 years, walking on the ground of sin which HE had cursed, to feel and experience His wrath, the consequence of disobedience.

7   Completing the redemptive work of Gen 3:21, by taking the sins of the world on Himself and pronounced on the cross: "It is finished" (John 19:30); and all things are new. Rev 21:5 "See, I am making all things new"... said the loud voice to John.

Wait a minute now; Changing mankind may take a long time for us, yes, but for GOD this is not the case, Matthew 19:26 says: "With people this is impossible, but with GOD all things are possible. Other reasons to delve into His Word include learning about His Love, Sacrifice and Purpose for mankind. John 3:16-17 "For GOD so loved the world, that He gave His only begotten Son, that whoever believes in Him shall not perish, but have eternal life. 17- For GOD did not send the Son into the world to judge the world, but that the world might be saved through Him"; 2 Peter 3:9 "The Lord is not slow about his promise, as some count slowness, but is patient toward you, not wishing for any to perish but for all to come to repentance".

The Word of GOD is true. The Word of GOD is the only truth. There is a lot of faith in the word of GOD. Jesus said in John 14:6 "I am the way, and the truth, and the life. No one comes to the Father except through me." That WORD of GOD has the power to pierce and cut our hearts, minds and souls, "Indeed the Word of GOD is living and active, sharper than any two-edged sword, piercing until it divides soul from spirit, joints from marrow; It is able to judge thoughts and intentions of the heart. And before Him no creature is hidden, but all are naked and laid bare to the eyes of the One to whom we must render an account". Hebrews 4:12,13 (NOAB). Yes indeed, everything is uncovered and stretched fully open to the eyes of the one to whom we must give account of ourselves (NJB)

For the Word of GOD is quick, and powerful, and sharper than any two-edged sword, piercing even to the dividing asunder of soul and spirit, and of the joints and marrow, and is a discerner of the thoughts and intents of the heart. Neither is there any creature that is not manifest in His sight: but all things are naked and opened unto the eyes of Him with whom we have to do. Hebrews 4:12,13 (KJV).

There are numerous lessons on patience from Genesis to Malachi according to the scriptures. The Lord came to live in the world physically for 33 years. He was sent to earth because something out of the ordinary was about to happen.

The Lord is about to fix things the way HE intended them to be. What is that something out of the ordinary that was about to happen? The regeneration of mankind once and for all. Matthew 3:2 "Repent for the kingdom of GOD is at hand." Matthew 4:17 "Repent, for the kingdom of GOD is at hand." Mark 1:14-15 "Now after John has been taken into custody, Jesus came into Galilee, preaching the Gospel of GOD. He said: "The time is fulfilled, and the kingdom of GOD is at hand; repent and believe in the gospel." But what is that something out of the ordinary that was about to be fulfilled or to happened? On the cross, Jesus was reconciling GOD with His creation through Him; (John 19:30 Jesus said: "it is finished") when absorbing the **wrath of GOD,** a new world and a new mankind start over. This may not be understood for those who are perishing, but for sinners who humble themselves to receive Him as Lord and Savior, ("to them He gave the right to become children of GOD" John 1:12) Good GOD almighty! GOD alone is GOD. Yes, GOD now has come to inhabit his believers. What a glory! Glory! Glory! Glory to GOD in the highest! Who can do this if it is not GOD alone.

The Bible is the only book that describes everything about this world, its past, its present and its future; and now, we are watching every day, and seeing all these truths being unfolding right before our eyes. Why an end? Would anybody like all the everyday things to continue forever the way they have been going on and the way they are going right now? Where the world has more wars, famine, hunger, disease, crime, fear, corruption, injustice etc... And things are escalating from bad to worse This is saddening and very troublesome for people to think that this present world should continue like it is forever. There are a very large group of people thinking that way; But it is written in II Timothy 3:1-5; *"You must understand this, that in the last days, distressing times will come. For people will be lovers of themselves, lovers of money, boasters, arrogant, abusive, disobedient to their parents, ungrateful, unholy, inhuman, implacable, slanderers, profligates, brutes, haters of good, treacherous, reckless, swollen with conceit, lovers of pleasure rather than lovers of God, holding to the outward form of godliness but denying its power. Avoid them" NOAB.* So, the same way that we read for fun, for learning, for education, for meditation, for remembering, and in a word for information etc..., it is also the same way the *"GLIMPSE Series"* would like the reader to get into reading the Bible for all the above reasons. The **GLIMPSE Series** starts with the first 3 chapters of the book of Genesis, and will come in three narratives or three books: one book for each chapter. Each will be challenging you to touch **that Bible**, to open it, to read it and, to meditate on it. If you are afraid to do so, it is because you don't want GOD to talk to you; but if you are not afraid, let's explore it. Let's go for the adventure. Yes, if you are serious to do so, I guarantee you that GOD will reveal Himself to you. Let's check it out. If you want to talk to GOD, He will talk back to you. HE will, yes, He will reveal HIMSELF to you:

Matthew7:7-8 "Ask, and it will be given to you; Seek, and you will find; Knock, and it will be opened to you. For everyone who asks receives, and he who seeks finds, and to him who knocks it will be opened." NASB

A word from my teacher to remember for you to always remember:

<u>*"When the student is ready; The teacher will appear.*</u>

PREFACE

The Bible -*filled with paradoxes*, is a compilation of 66 books written by different authors, about 40- not at the same time, but over a period of time; they are prophets, cupbearers, priests, shepherds, fishermen and even a military general. The Bible is the only book in the world that describes and narrate a beginning of time and, an end of time. It contains the history of the world and its future.

According to the preface of a (KJV) King James Version of the Bible copyrighted in 1948 (from other previous copyrights dated 1926, 1928, 1930, 1938, 1941 by THE JOHN A. HERTEL. CO.) "The Bible is a library of Divine Truth. It is the masterpiece of all literature. Its truths have been the world's greatest achievements in literature, sculpture, art, science, and in reform and inspirational teaching. It is the supreme authority on practical knowledge for men and women in every walk of life. Within its sacred pages may be found counsel and wisdom for every condition and circumstance of human experience. its scope is broader than all human knowledge and experience, and its heights and depths reach beyond the utmost limits of all eternities".

The intent of this book is to take everyone who loves to read, to consider its message, reflect deeply on it, and take it for what it says. The Bible may be too voluminous to read but each book of it has its own message, mystery, objective, information and lesson. Many have said it is incomplete and has a lot of flows and inaccuracies. And according to the gospel of John 21:25 it is said: 'And there are also many other things which Jesus did, which if they were written in detail,... That is okay but, there is a great message in it that is undeniable: "John 3:16-17". Please check Genesis 1, John 1, Matthew 1:23-25, Genesis 3:21, Isaiah 51, Isaiah 61:1-3, Matthew 3:2-3, Matthew 4:17, Mark 1:4, Mark 1:14-15, Luke 2:9-10, Luke 16:19-31, Luke 23:44, John 19:30, Matthew 28, Matthew 16, Luke 21, Luke 24 etc...

This book is about the first chapter of the book of GENESIS in the Bible, a narrative on the beginning of the world; its creation. The second chapter will be a second book and will explore another view of creation, which is how man was created. And the third book will visit the fall of mankind. It is neither a commentary, a bible dictionary, nor an encyclopedia. The content may startle and provoke many readers; it may also be controversial, loathsome, nonsense, grotesque, incomprehensible and plausible for some, a blessing for others. The exegesis may also be very hard for many readers, but it is *just the way I see it and understand it*. One can just take it, read it and believe it; One can do all three and also wants to know more. One does not have to agree with how I see it and understand it; however, one must also wonder; what if it is all true, what is my fate? Why Should I read the Bible? What is in it for me?

As I understand it, I am depicting a broader view behind the curtains of the beginning of the world and the fall of mankind through the Bible alone. I would like you to know that this type of work will attempt to interpret the reality and the significance of the creation of the world (Not a big bang theory). Remember the big purpose behind it is for you to check the Bible out, for you to read your Bible.

In the introduction of the book of Genesis by the NOAB (New Oxford Annotated Bible) pages 9-10, it is said that "...most scholars now recognize that Genesis is a postexilic combination of two bodies of material":

1- A 'Priestly' editorial or source beginning with the seven-day creation account in Gen 1:1-2:3 and,
2- A 'non-Priestly' source beginning with the garden of Eden story in Gen 2:4-3:24."

In this series, as we are being curious, we are going to revisit, explore, consider and try to understand what was going on, and what went on (although we may not understand a lot for now). What is in there to learn? What is in there to know? There is a lot to learn and to know, because the truth resides in the Bible. ***__The truth is in the Bible,__*** and the Son of GOD is the embodiment of the truth; "For in Him all the fullness of Deity dwells in bodily form" (Colossians 2:9). You have mostly heard, and are probably used to hearing pastors, preachers, ministers, evangelists and theologians saying that the Word of GOD is pregnant with meanings. Indeed, there's a lot to know about the Word of GOD or this great GOD whom one day; we will finally be able to see face to face. ***Face to face?*** *Yes. Face to* *face*. But the belief was that no one can see GOD and live. Well Hagar said it Genesis 16:13. Why did she say that? Was there such belief? How can she say such thing if there were not such belief? How can we know such if we do not <u>read, meditate and study our Bible</u>? Hold on! Wait a minute now. The Lord declared to Moses (Exodus 33:20)…"for no man can see me and live!" Exodus 33:11 said: "Thus the Lord used to speak to Moses face to face, just like a man speaks to his friend". WOW! What is all that already? But GOD also appeared in many other forms to people such as: Burning bush (Ex 3:2); Pillar of cloud (13:21) (Numbers 12:5) "then the Lord came down in a pillar of cloud and stood at the doorway…" ; pillar of fire by night etc… but, do we or will we really know what happened in the beginning? *By faith, yes*. Maybe we shouldn't have asked the question like that and answered it too quick but, there are a few reasons for the question. The only major piece of evidence we have is: The Pentateuch, The Hebrew Bible, The Torah, The Bible, and the story that is written in it. No other book has painted the beginning of the world in such fashion and details. The information is direct, crisp, concrete, true and established. Now, as far as the rest of the Bible (including the New Testament) has talked about the creation of the world: Isaiah 45:18, Job 38, Psalms 33:6, 89:12, 136:5-9, Acts14:15, 17:24, Colossians1:16 etc… Meanwhile HE is with us. He is inside of us, we are in HIM; please read John 17:21-23. (We will get back to the "face to face"), But how could this be? The belief (of someone seeing GOD and staying alive) is confirmed first in Genesis 16:13 with Hagar, the slave servant of Sarai; but read the whole chapter 16 for a better understanding; also in Exodus 33:20 where, no one can see GOD's face and live; however the belief existed before because, Abraham, Sarah, Hagar, Isaac, Jacob, Moses, Aaron, Miriam, Isaiah, Solomon, Isaiah, Gideon, Joshua, Jephthah and many more had seen the Lord GOD. Some of them wondered why they were still alive; but when they saw the Lord, they worshiped Him. The Bible describes that at many occasions that GOD appeared to Abraham, Hagar (not in all of His glory off course) Gen 12:7, 14:17-20, 17:1, 17:22, 18:1-33, Exodus 4:1, as for Hagar Gen 16:7-13 who believed she will not live because she had seen the Lord. Many had this privilege to see GOD in a temporary form and still live; sometimes as an Angel (whom accept worship, angels don't accept worship Rev 19:10) sometimes in other forms. The manifestation of GOD in a temporary form to humans is called *"Theophany"*; that is the word that explains such awesome and extraordinary epiphany. To conclude, we would like to add that in the past, when GOD was talking to man, there was no mediator at that time, so GOD had to reveal HIMSELF in some kind of way to anyone who pleases Him or to anyone He wanted to show Himself to; and one last reference to support this is found in the book of Exodus, chapter 6 verses 2,3: "And Elohim spoke unto Moshe, and said unto him, I am Hashem; And I appeared unto Avraham, unto Yitzchak and unto Ya'akov, as El Shaddai, but by my Shem Hashem I did not make Myself known to them" (OJB). GOD also spoke to Moses and said to him: I am the LORD. I appeared to Abraham, Isaac, and Jacob as GOD Almighty, but by my name 'The Lord' I did not make myself known to them (NOAB); ***but what is it that is in us that please GOD?***

And finally, the Word was made flesh. WOW! WOW! How can this be? Wait a minute now. GOD was the Word, becoming flesh. And dwelt among us. <u>Spiritual</u> and <u>natural</u>. WOW! And the Word incarnated in the person of Jesus, the Christ. The Son of the living GOD. Indeed, the Lord came and dwelt among mortals in order to become mortal to fix this mess (Remember Genesis 3:21, Hallelujah!!!) HE bathed them and washed them in the blood of the Lamb, and dressed them with its skin. Now since His holiness is such a raging fire, since HE has to show respect to His own word (Good GOD Almighty), The Lord then touched sin.

Let Us make man... WOW! (Does that ring a bell?) Mystery, mystery, mystery for those who are perishing but, for those who believe and have received HIM... this mystery is revealed. (verses 12 & 13 of John 1).

1- Please read John 1:1-14 "In the beginning was the Word, and the Word was with GOD, and the Word was GOD.
2- He was in the beginning with GOD.
3- All things came into being through HIM, and apart from HIM nothing came into being that has come into being.
4- In HIM was life, and the Life was the light of men.
5- The Light shines in the darkness, and the darkness did not comprehend it.
6- There came a man sent from GOD, whose name was John.
7- He came as a witness to testify about the Light, so that all might believe through HIM.

8- He was not the Light, but he came to testify about the Light.

9- There was the true Light which, coming into the world, enlightens every man.

10- HE was in the world, and the world was made through HIM, and the world did not know HIM.

11- HE came to His own, and those who were His own did not receive HIM.

12- But as many as receive HIM, to them HE gave the right to become children of GOD, even to those who believe in HIS name,

13- who were born, not of blood nor of the will of the flesh nor of the will of man, but of GOD.

14- And the WORD became flesh, and dwelt among us, and we saw HIS glory, glory as of the only begotten from the Father, full of grace and truth." And one more, the creator of all things, Colossians1:16, GOD calling the Lord GOD, GOD calling Jesus, GOD Hebrews 1:1-14, Psalms 45:6-7

But how can we answer these questions? What is it that is in us that pleases God that after man disobeyed HIM, since He damned him to die, but found a way to rescue him, Gen 3:21. Who is this GOD? How can this be? I personally have no further questions.

FOREWORD

Can we understand the mind of GOD? Can we really know GOD? Can we really know what's in the mind of GOD? We cannot even dare going there because HE created us, but how can we know GOD? How can we know this GOD? Please read John 15:1-11

"IF ONE SAYS THAT HE OR SHE BELIEVES IN GOD AND DOES NOT BELIEVE IN HIS WORD AND HIS CREATION, HIS OR HER BELIEF IS FUTILE". (FP 7-28-15)

So this booklet is not telling anything new about the Bible except that it is going to approach the creation of the world and the fall of mankind very simply, and see how the Bible itself explains everything we need to know so far. It will also show that some of what you have heard is also in the Bible and some others are not. The Bible presents GOD in all of His power and might but also as a very loving, kind responsible and respectful Father; just and stern, caring for everything He has done and for His creation, also very concerned for the well-being of Adam and Eve and HIS plan (Gen2:18), (Gen3:8-21). The great character of GOD is very well tangible and visible in His creation.

Regardless of countless researches and findings that scientists, religious scholars and researchers have found about the world; this world and the heavens, the Bible **is** and **remains** the only book among all other books, that starts with the history of the world, its beginning, its end, how it all began and how it will end for a forever life with GOD. (Gen 1:1 "In the beginning when GOD... or In the beginning GOD... and Rev 21:1 "And I saw a new heaven and a new earth... or Then I saw a new heaven and a new earth..."). What do all these things tell us? **The Bible is not a religious book**. Some people tried to make it so. The Bible is a relationship book between GOD and man. We can see from space scientific research pictures and videos other planets but, we never see life on them or living beings on them. Who knows? "**GOD is Spirit**" said Jesus to the Samaritan woman in John 4:24. The image of the invisible GOD... Colossians1:15. Are the angels visible or invisible sometimes? They are visible the majority of the time. The history and future are combined in that book where a man comes and declares He's the Son of man, and He is the Son of GOD:

- He is the Son of man (Mark 2:10, John 5:27, Matthew 11:19, Luke 9:56);
- He is the Son of GOD (Matthew 11:27; 27:43; Luke 10:22, John 5:22, 25), the creator of the world (Jesus Christ the Word, becoming flesh and dwelt among us John 1:14, Job 38:4, Isaiah 41:20, 42:5; and that HIM

and GOD are one, and finally that, He is the only way to GOD John 14:6-10. What is all this? When JESUS CHRIST, the Son of the living GOD declares in Matt 24:35, Mark 13:31, and Luke 21:31 that: "Heaven and Earth will pass away, but my words will not pass away". If He is not the Alpha and Omega, the first and the last then, who is He? He was declaring WHO HE really IS, reminding to those who were around Him at that time about the veracity of who was among them and, emphasizing on the authenticity of the truth: The Word of GOD; The Word of God is true, and the Word of God is the only truth (John 17:17). When He was ministering on the earth, he always refers the Scribes and the Pharisees to the scriptures (Matthew 15:8,9; 21:42; Mark 12:36; 14:27; Luke 7:27; 18:20; 20: 34-44); Because, very often He will say to them: "it is written or Haven't you read"... There is an order in the bible. Everything is already written. Everything. We are not even trying to bring explanations, definitions and significances to the first three chapters of the book of *Genesis* however, all we are trying to do is to bring people to read the Bible, study the Bible, take into great consideration the narrative and the message, to stop and think, and see what this Bible is telling us, and finally see this book in another angle that reveal this great GOD. We may sound very redundant but, if you really like to read, the view will make you wonder, want to study more and want to know more. The Bible will hurt your mind, your soul and your heart because of its message. So, after many researches and extensive readings, we are not saying that we will bring definitions, explanations, and more significances of these three (3) chapters of the book of Genesis but, we can however say that this glimpse of these eighty (80) verses as we understand them, will change your perspective about this great GOD who, relentlessly never ceases, to call mankind back to him. This GOD, who respects your **free will** and **let you take charge of your** **destiny,** who also will make you wonder; "In Luke 8:22-25, Mark 4:35-41 where a great windstorm arose, and waves were beating into the boat while the Master went for a nap. The disciples got so scared that they woke Him up. He woke up and rebuked the wind in saying: Peace! Be Still!" And in verse 41 of Mark 4: The disciples said to one another "Who then is this, that even the wind and the sea obey him"; but in verse 25 of Luke chapter 8, it's more assertive; "Who then is this, that even the winds and the water, and they obey Him". GOD in flesh, "and the Word became flesh, and dwelt among us... John 1:14". Amazement in (Matthew 8:23-27) got them saying: "What kind of man is this, that even the winds and the sea obey Him." These are things that when you read them, you should have been in awe, picturing these phenomena in your mind and wonder. Consider the disciples who were human being like you and I, who witnessed these things; seeing the lame and the paralytic walking, the blind seeing, the dead raised, etc... So, the goal of this book is to bring and get more people to take a deeper look at the Bible, to read it and study it. We are appealing to the readers to consider and reconsider the narrative and the scenario again, again and again at another level so that they have a better understanding of who GOD is and what is his plan and purpose for us. Hoping that these minutes you will spend in the words of this booklet will be a blessing and that by reading your bible, God will bless you to a hundred-fold in the study of his word. As we mentioned previously...

THE BEGINNING OF THE WORLD IS GREAT AND PERFECT, GOD HAD A SPECIFIC PLAN FOR MANKIND, BUT SIN AND DEATH GOT INTO IT. DID GOD MAKE A MISTAKE? DID HE MISS SOMETHING? CAN WE SAY SO? NO.

N.B. Lastly, we will be using different versions or translations of the Bible: OJB, KJV, NOAB, NASB, Amplified, NLT, etc... But the main versions utilized in these series will be mostly the NOAB, the NASB and the NJB. Whatever the version of the Bible that you are reading, please have at least a Bible with you when you are reading this book. Don't forget. This is just a glimpse, just a glimpse of the Word GOD and the power of GOD.

AMPC: Amplified Bible, Classic Edition

OJB: Orthodox Jewish Bible

KJV: King James Version

NOAB: New Oxford Annotated Bible (with the Apocrypha)

NRSVA: New Revised Standard Version Anglicized

NRSV: New Revised Standard Version

NASB: New American Standard Bible

NJV: New Jerusalem Bible

WARNING!

There are many assumptions in these writings however, they are written in the objective of having the reader to see the beginning of the work of GOD (Can we say so?) in another dimension. Can we know without knowledge? It doesn't mean that GOD has a beginning. (GOD was before the beginning of the world. In the beginning was the Word, John 1:1. The Word was before the beginning of the world; The Word was there... John17:5). <u>We don't know how long and the amount of time when GOD was but, GOD IS.</u> (Please read Exodus 3, John 8). The time of the beginning is completely unknown. Can we know without being taught or without studying, reading? Can we know without hearing? Can we know without researching and looking? Can we know without experiencing? Can we know without understanding? <u>Understand then and know what you believe in.</u> Why would Jesus Christ say to the Pharisees: "Have ye not read"... (Matt 19:4&5) if reading were not important? A lot of people assume that our ancestors (Adam & Eve) didn't know anything, but they were being taught and instructed by GOD. Here is GOD almighty, in His creation of the world and the living in it, and one would come with the question of Adam and Eve did not know how to read; how absurd is that? GOD created a replica of Himself (Gen 1:26)? We understand that, but common sense also will make you *see that particular assumption another way. Why? As we see it, when GOD created man, he stared imparting some knowledge to him (Gen 2:19-20). HE brought animals to him to see what he would call them; ...And whatever Adam called every living creature, that was its name. <u>Remember </u>that GOD created them in His image and likeness. And what about Noah? Well, what about Noah? How did Noah know about taking measurements when GOD was giving instruction to him about the size and how to build the Arc, Gen 6:15-16?* GOD created us smart, beautiful and gave us knowledge; we just failed to use our understanding and stay in communion with Him. Were we afraid or were we doubtful? Well we asked such questions because of what's coming up in Genesis 2:18 Then the Lord GOD said, "It is **not good** that the man should be alone; I will make him a helper suitable for him." Was something missing?The Lord GOD did foresee Adam's loneliness. The Bible starts with a strong affirmation that is plain and simple, "In the beginning, GOD created the heavens and the earth". That's what it was in the beginning and that's how it was.

The book will bounce you (the reader) from time to time to many references in the Bible. It is written that way in order to make you participate in that small study of these 3 chapters. They are referred to the reader so that he or she can really go and check everything out. These references explain a great deal of what went on in the beginning (we believe there was more that words were not able to express or describe, but by faith we accept what we read) or can we say, that these verses are trying to expand and open our mind to the infinite greatness of GOD. It is very important to remember the exegesis may not be too easy to accept and understand; but just consider it.

In conclusion, 1 Corinthians 3:10-11; the apostle Paul wrote: "According to the grace of GOD which was given to me, like a wise master I laid a foundation, and another is building on it. But each man must be careful how he builds on it. For no man can lay a foundation other than the one which is laid, which is **JESUS CHRIST**." (Good GOD Almighty! The Son of the living GOD). Yes. And Paul is right. The one laid by JESUS, The Christ. (Good GOD Almighty! The Son of the living GOD). The only essence of life, the only door, the only way to the Father. (John 14:6).

Genesis.

What is the etymology of this word? What does it mean?

Genesis- The first book of the Hebrew bible, The Pentateuch, The Torah, The Tanakh, The Christian Old Testament.

It is a name coming from the Greek that signifies the original, generation or beget; bringing into existence or being, the source, the beginning, the origin of something. In conclusion, it's the origin or the beginning of what we are seeing today. The Expository Dictionary of the Bible defines the word "Genesis" like this: "genesis is a rare noun denoting the "genealogy" of Jesus Christ in Matthew 1:1.

<u>-The word Genesis (a Hebrew word) meaning "In the beginning"- It's the first book of the Hebrew Bible.</u>

As far as the author of the book, there is assumption that the book of Genesis could have been written during the 40 year period of wandering of the Israelites in the desert from 1446-1406 B.C. or 1491-1451 B.C., by Moses however, it is said that old writings and ancient manuscripts cannot show sufficient proof of authorship about the book. It's been called: "The first book of the Torah or the Pentateuch. We want to make one thing clear here. Moses was talking to the Israelites and pointed an important fact to the people in Deuteronomy 4:19 "And when you look up to the heavens and see the sun, the moon, the stars, all the host of heaven, do not be led astray and bow down to them and serve them - one of the things that Moses meant was that these creations make one wonders indeed, but there is GOD in heaven who created them— those which the Lord your GOD has allotted to all the peoples everywhere under heaven".

Well, why would Moses say such things if (1) these things about the creation of the world were not revealed to him or written earlier somewhere; (2) if they were not revealed to him or to someone before him, who knows? It is written according to Exodus 24:4 "And Moses wrote all the words of the Lord...", but one thing is certain: If Jewish and Christian scholars alike have attributed the authorship to Moses, this is one reference that gives more strength to their assumption. Is Moses really the author? What can we say? We do not know; before they published their findings, they have done deep extensive research of historic places, old documents, hieroglyphic tablets etc... which convinced them to attribute the authorship to him. Or what if it were a custom that there was a constant clerk or secretary, who was there literally just to report or write down everything that was going on at that time, and that was passed from generation to generation (that may have been his constant job; remember also the tribe of Levi) specifically to record every detail, events or any little thing that were going on at that time or all spiritual and religious matters. Another thing to consider is that Moses was probably one of the most educated people during his time (I am not saying there were not other educated men at that time) since he was raised as a son to Pharaoh's daughter (Exodus 2:10-11). The guy was considered a prince. If he had stayed there, we probably would have had the story of the beginning or the Israelites another way, but I wouldn't even go too far with that concept, because when GOD chooses you to do something, HE knows you can do it according to what HE envisions. Favor? Some kind of favor? Bizarre kind of favor. And he happened to talk to GOD like a man talked to his friend (Exodus 33:11) There's an estimated 35 years in the palace by historians but since he was the Princess' son (by adoption of course), he probably received the best education possible. However, in verse 22 and 23 in chapter 7 in the book of Acts, Luke reported that Moses was educated in all learning of the Egyptians. Luke probably had something we didn't have. *Always remember to consider and reconsider; because what if history may have been transmitted by not only by word of mouth alone but also by those who heard it and transmitted it through writings. In plain common sense, that's what it was. The elders may have had historians among them who recorded GOD's revelation, precepts, rules and events, in other religious books that are not in the Bible etc... then came also the question of authenticity. There are so many books that report the creation of heaven and earth, and other events of the Bible. There are the books of Jasher, Jubilee, Enoch etc...* What about the 12 tribes? What about them? Well remember that portion of lands were given to 11 of them, but one tribe (Joshua 18:7 For the Levites have no portion among you, because the priesthood of the Lord is their inheritance) did not receive a portion of land and had a specific assignment; The Levi tribe, (Levi, the 3rd son of Leah and Jacob, Genesis 29:34) the Levites are distinguished by being consecrated to do GOD's work for the Israelites and in the Temple. Remember, the 12 tribes are named after the sons of Jacob, whose name was changed to Israel (Genesis 32:28). When Moses went and spent forty days and forty nights on Mount Sinai (Exodus 24:18), there are a lot of things that the Bible does not report or tell or relate about what was going on up there on the mountain. The Bible only reported about the ordinances and commandments that the Lord gave to him and that's spelled out from Exodus 19 through chapter 31 (plenty of paradoxes here). Now, let us consider a few things: read again the first twelve verses up to verse fifteen of chapter 24 again, where the almighty GOD allow Moses and the (70) seventy elders of Israel to see HIM; where they ate and they drank (*Meanwhile no one can see GOD and live*). The Lord was constantly in conversation with Moses; sometimes in one form or another or it seems like most of the times it's like HE is in Moses' head talking or next to him talking. Well do not ask me. Find it out. How? By reading your Bible; there's plenty of blessings in reading the word of the Lord.

Then Moses would transmit the message of GOD (Ex 19-23) to the people, and furthermore, HE (GOD) is about to show up among Moses and the elders (Ex 24:9-11), with just a glimpse of His Glory, to eat, drink and dine with Moses and the elders. Eat and drink and dine with the Lord? Moses would spend 40 days and 40 nights, just to have the commandments and the ordinances? Come on! We believe (only me, I do not know about you) that Moses spent 960 hours very busy, in the presence of the Lord, not just to receive the ordinances and the commandments. I also believe that He was so busy in the presence of GOD that days and nights didn't matter. That's acceptable and we can agree with that; but, we would agree more if from all these things that the Lord will dictate to Moses, starting from the end of chapter 24:15-18 and (Ex 25 through 31) that he spent forty days and forty nights to take all of this information? Then Moses was very busy up there; either taking dictation and writing down what GOD was telling him to write (since he was very well-educated Acts 7:22) or contemplating the fingers of GOD writing the law and the ordinances to him, maybe telling him about how he began creation, but also *enjoying the presence of the Lord.* However, in **the book of Jubilee**, page 39 chapter 1, beginning in verse 27 where GOD commanded an angel to write for Moses about the new creation of the world. There are also so many assumptions that we can make but we have to stay in the spirit of this book.

It is agreed among religious scholars, researchers, theologians and scientists that there are two different accounts about the creation of the world before the fall of man: Genesis 1 is one account; and Genesis 2 is another account; that there are also two types of stories in the book. There is a primeval history from chapters 1-11, and an ancestral history from chapters 12-50 (Wikipedia), but we are just going to stay in the first chapter for right now.

Very Important... We may have a gazillion questions about the creation of the world, the heavens, and the beginning however, there is also an assumption of what is being called a "gap theory". What is "the Gap Theory"? This question is answered in the coming epilogue of verse 1. But it is written in the Bible about a war that broke out in heavens in Revelation 12:1-9, and also where in chapter 4 of the book of Jeremiah, from verses 23 thru 28, something happened. The foot note in the NOAB Bible said: "In a vision, the prophet sees the terrifying results of GOD's irrevocable judgment, but in Isaiah 7:14-16, the Prophet prophesied about the child who was to be born from the woman who was with child, and that he would eat curds and honey. We know that it is said Matthew 3:4 that John the Baptist food was eating "locusts and wild honey". Is there anywhere else in the Bible that show that Jesus was fed with curds and honey? The name of the child shall be Immanuel, meaning "GOD with us". Did He ever eat curds and honey? But that's what the Prophet said. We also know that when He was tempted after 40 days and 40 nights, after He rebuked the devil, angels came and ministered to Him (Matthew 4:11). And since angels came and ministered to Him, maybe they brought Him curds and honey or maybe they brought Him something else to eat. After all, this is GOD' Son. He just finished 40 days and 40 nights without food. There's not a passage, nor a verse which said that he ate something after these forty days. Does that mean that there were other things in the beginning or before the beginning? Can we venture there? Yes. with the Bible in hand and in our heads and hearts. Now someone may think about John the Baptist, because the Bible reveals that his food was locusts and honey in Matthew 3:4. We have so many unanswered questions: From eight days after Jesus' circumcision, after Joseph and Mary had finished doing everything the Law of the Lord required (Luke 2:39,40)we have 11 years of Jesus growing in maturity and being filled with wisdom, and GOD's favor was with Him. The next thing we know, Jesus is 12 years old and was missing for a few days (3 days, verse 46) at the feast of the Passover. Does it say where He was? Don't ask me; Verse 40 gave the answer, but from 12 years of age until being around 30 years of age, we have no information. If we go in the very beginning of the world, we have less information because we can only rely on that revelation which the Bible presents and some other information that other books provided; but we have to read them with common sense. Like in the book of Jubilee, an angel is appointed to give Moses the story of the creation of the world. In conclusion, my recommendations remain the same: read your bible, ask the Lord to open your minds and hearts to understand the writings in it. I guarantee it will be good for your souls; for some who do a a lot of research on social media, don't stop looking for information, but you should know this. If that man came, claiming He is the Son of GOD, and that no one has ever seen GOD, that

Him and GOD (the Father) are one (John 14:6-21), that He heals the sick, raise the dead, make the leper clean again, predicted his death, died, and was resurrected the third day, and declared and commissioned His believers in Matthew 28:18-20 by saying: "All authority in heaven and on earth has been given to me. Go therefore and make disciples of all nations, baptizing them in the name of the Father and of the Son and of the Holy Spirit, and teaching them to obey everything that I have commanded you. And remember, I am with you always, to the end of the age." (NOAB). So, it's all in the Bible, and it's all in the beginning. Yes! Everything is in the beginning. The followings are two types of outlines of chapter 1:

Verses 1-2, the beginning.???

Verses 3-5, first day, creation of light.

Verses 6-8, second day, creation of the great expanse or dome or firmament

Verses 9-13, third day, the creation of dry land.

Verses 14-19, fourth day, creation of the sun, the moon and the stars.

Verses 20-23, fifth day, creation of birds and sea creatures.

Verses 24-31, sixth day, land creatures, mankind.

1- The creation of heaven and earth
2-   "   of the light. 1ˢᵗ day.

3-	"	of the firmament. 2nd day.

3-   "   of the firmament. 2<u>nd</u> day.

4-   "   of the earth separated from the waters. 3<u>rd</u> day. (dry ground)

5-   "   of the fruitfulness of the earth. 3rd day also.

6-   "   of the sun, moon and stars. 4<u>th</u> day.

7-   "   of fish and fowl. 5<u>th</u> day.

8-   "   of beast and cattle. 6<u>th</u> day. Creatures on land.

9-   "   of man in the image of GOD. 6th day also. Creation of man.

10- The appointment of food

❧ Chapter 1, Verse 1-2 ❧

-In the beginning when GOD created the heaven and the earth, the earth was a formless void and darkness covered the face of the deep, while a wind from GOD swept over the face of the waters.(NOAB)

In the beginning Elohim created hashomayim (the heavens, Himel) and haaretz (the earth.)And the earth was tohu vavohu (without form, and void); and darkness was upon the face of the deep. And the Ruach Elohim was hovering upon the face of the waters. (OJB)

-In the beginning GOD created the heavens and the earth. The earth was formless and void, and darkness was over the surface of the deep, and the Spirit of GOD was moving over the surface of the waters. (NASB)

In the beginning GOD(Spirit. John 4:24 "GOD is spirit) the Word, was the Word (John 1:1) and the Word was with GOD (John 14:7), and the Word was GOD.

- Jeremiah 10:10 "... But the Lord is the true GOD, HE is the living GOD, and an everlasting King".
  Are there other gods? Yes, but they did not create heaven and earth
- Jeremiah 10:12 "He hath made the earth by his power, He hath established the World by His Wisdom, and hath stretched out the heavens by his discretion."
- Job, chapters 38 and 39 talk about the creation, but what does the beginning of the world have to do with Job? Well, these two chapters have a lot to do with the beginning.

In the beginning GOD...: Isaiah 44:6 "Thus said the Lord, the King of Israel and his Redeemer, the Lord of hosts: I am the first and I am the last. And there is no GOD besides Me." Here are a few other ones: Revelation 22:13 "I am the Alpha and the Omega, the first and the last, the beginning and the end". Revelation 21:6 Then He said to me: "It is done. I am the Alpha and the Omega, the beginning and the end"... Why would Jesus call Himself the beginning and the end? Was He saying He is GOD?... Moses was teaching the Israelites as follows: "Hear, O Israel! The Lord is our GOD, the Lord is one." And the Lord Jesus Christ repeated it in Mark 12:29; it will be also wise to go and read verses 18 through 34. Check these verses out.

So, at that particular time (in the beginning), at this specific period in GOD's bosom or mind. In GOD's own knowledge alone. A period or a time that is completely unknown to us; or it may have been after the time that GOD was doing a bunch of other stuff, because the beginning focused on the heaven (which we just have an idea of what it is constituted of), and the earth which we live on now. This time was before things started being distinguished, showing appearance, shall I say characterizing, put in place and order. Please consider: in Job 38 through 41, especially chapters 40 and 41 where this reading will take your breath away, during Job's calamity, hoping that most Christians know the story of Job. If not, we would like to invite you to read it and come back to this book; where GOD Himself came in a whirlwind is talking to Job, to let him know about certain mysteries for mankind about the creation of the world. Mysteries about the foundation of the world, the personality and the character of God; but what does the beginning have to do with the book of Job? Well, in that part of the bible, God was lecturing Job about who HE is, His character, His personality, His power, His glory, and the glory of His creation. In the beginning, at that particular period of time; which is not a daily counted time as we will soon see in verse 5 with day and night. In other words; it is a specific time or a period that is only in the awareness and the understanding of GOD alone, nevertheless is absolutely and completely not within our knowledge and understanding or comprehension. (Probably way before anything else or before all things came to be.) Even if we say that, we cannot bring a more concrete and a real time table to this assumption.

Another thing to think about when GOD was lecturing Job is: GOD is talking about foundation. Foundation? Yes. Foundation, because GOD said to Job in the 38th chapter at the 4th verse: "Where were you when I laid the foundation of the earth"?... Really! So, the earth is sitting on nothing.

Is there something holing it? Is faith there? Almost everyone understands that, however, the beginning could have been way before everything was or started-such as life, action, and movement start etc or even before there was any action or mention of time; when there was absolutely no time frame, but a lot of other things may have happened before the beginning or during the beginning (meaning how the beginning is being unfolded), or after the beginning???. Another way of seeing it is that <u>time may have started right there and then</u>, because it says "in the beginning". But we still cannot say that for many reasons one of them is that we were not there.

Now, is there a length of time in the beginning? We don't know, but it seems that there is not; on the same token, there's nothing wrong to question these assumptions, because another type of time will start in verse 5, when God began to create (Gen 1:1...The Heavens) the universe. He created many heavens. In the majority of the bible translations, it is said: "God created the Heavens (plural) and the earth". That is what He created in the beginning. (hold that thought). The (NOAB) "New Oxford Annotated Bible" reports the beginning like this: ***In the beginning when God created the heavens and the earth,...*** probably meaning (when GOD created it, this is how it was. This is what happened)... And verse 2 is linked up to it or moved to how, the state of the earth was. With the word was... by continuing like this: the earth was a formless void and darkness etc... And the story begins... the account starts to unfold. And the first account begins... with the description of how the earth was and the description of how GOD started to create things now on the earth and around the earth. With that being said, which also means that before the beginning, there might have had been other things (That's where the gap theorists tried to score a point) other than the earth. Can we jump from here to Jeremiah 4:20-28. Something happened. Can you find out? Can we find out then? Please check also (jewishvirtuallibrary.org "Creation and Cosmogony in the Bible". this version of the Bible (the NOAB) does not end verse 1 with a (.) period, we mean a dot in punctuation like the majority of other versions do but, continues verse 1 with a (,) coma to verse 2; That is one of the reasons why we said that the gap theory does not make sense. There is absolutely no Gap Theory in the NOAB version or (NRSVA) according to the 1st chapter of Genesis 1:1 and 2. Another view to consider is in the (NJB) New Jerusalem Bible, because verses 1 & 2 said: In the beginning GOD created heaven and earth. (2) Now the earth was a formless void, there was darkness over the deep, with a divine wind sweeping over the waters. Notice the simplicity of the beginning of GOD's creation in both verse 1 and 2. In verse 2, the author is explaining by being very descriptive of how it happened in saying the word "Now". That is one of the reasons why I would like some of you to see that whether there is a period or a coma at the end of verse 1; there is still a connection between the two verses, because verse 2 starts to unfold the account or explains how everything was.

Now, most other versions start like this: "In the beginning, GOD created the heaven (some say Heavens) and the earth". And probably, because of this sentence -since it ends with a period- there are a great number of bible scholars that came up with a theory called "the gap theory". The (tgp) called "*the gap theory*". What is "The Gap Theory"? Well, the gap theory is the belief by some scholars and theologians came out with by saying that there is a lapse of time in Genesis 1:1 and 1:2. They are stating there is a separation of time, events and things. That period (the dot) that separates verse 1 and verse 2 is very profound and significant. And according to them, verse 1 denote that GOD created heaven and earth and everything was great and beautiful at a certain time, so with that dot which is in most different Bible versions after verse 1, is not in the (NOAB) Bible and also means that something happened. According to them, Lucifer decided to go or went for a Coup d'Etat, and GOD and His angels kicked them out of heaven to the earth, under the leadership of Michael; since there was no place in heaven for them (Rev 12:7-9). That is where their assumption makes no sense. This is also where we can also come with other assumptions to counteract their concept. Now remember brethren, the word of GOD stands strong. GOD created the world with His word. Let us be more specific: Hebrews 11:3 says "By faith we understand that the worlds were prepared by the word of GOD"... Palms 33:6 said: "by the word of the Lord the heavens were made, and by the breath of His mouth all their host."

If you are researching on the internet, you will find quite a vast selection of that theory. They tried to make it biblical but, there is not enough evidence to support it. However, the point we tried to make (with NOAB version) is that there is no place for the gap; but the other versions give suspicious heed to that assumption with just a dot. That's another argument that we cannot have in this book. Some major references for the gap theory could have been also: Isaiah 13:13, and Isaiah 24:1-6, Jeremiah 4:20-28, 2 Peter 3. But one would believe they would support their argument with Revelation 12:7-9. Verse 9 said the dragon was thrown... Notice the past tense "was"...That's another great discussion for another time. Remember the word "***paradox***", verse 8 ... shows that there was no place in heaven anymore for the dragon and his angels and verse 9 said they were thrown down to the earth. Who knows, maybe that was GOD's plan to check out the knowledge and the judgment -the thinking- of Adam and Eve. Now this is an argument that could have been used for the gap theory and since GOD has already reserved judgment and condemnation forever in the lake of fire for Satan and his angels (Rev 19:20, Rev 20:10, Rev 14:9-11, Daniel 7:11. So the gap theorists could have also come with that argument since they were cast out down to the earth, and meanwhile, GOD decided to create something new in the face of Lucifer after a technical knock-out (TKO) for seven days; he showed that His Word stands, and that He is building this universe according to what He has in mind, to live in harmony with His will, care and love forever. Why would Jesus remind the devil during the temptation (Matthew 4:7) "Again it is written, do not put the Lord your GOD to the test." <u>The Lord your GOD</u>. Jesus said to him, meaning (I have created you.) you are and will be under my control. now the mind-blowing part of this is that Satan knows the power of the Word. there is so, so, so much to say here. WOW!!! The gap theory makes just a little sense in most Bible versions, but does not make sense at all in the NOAB. In other words, the evidence that is missing is that time.

GOD: [El Ohim]. Yes, GOD. In Hebrew the word is plural. That's the GOD with great and awesome power and might. The El-Shaddai GOD. The Lord GOD almighty in tandem with JESUS CHRIST, the WORD; and the Holy Spirit. O what a mystery!!! If you accept it by faith, light will shine in your spirit to start understanding what is hidden for the most intelligent people in the world. John 1:1 "in the beginning was the Word, and the Word was with GOD, and the Word was GOD" (some may not agree with this due to unbelief). The Creator (Elohim), the Eternal Word, takes action, creates the heavens and the earth. He is the maker of heaven and earth. Psalms 33:6 "by the Word of the Lord, the heavens were made. We cannot be more explanatory than this.

In Genesis 14:18-20 we are introduced to Melchizedek, Priest of GOD [El Elyon]Most High (the name means "King of Righteousness"); there is only one King of Righteousness. That alone should shake you all the way to the bones. Salem is a name for Jerusalem; Jerusalem is the city of the Great King; with Abraham, they blessed the Most High God, (19) they called HIM, Possessor or Maker of heaven and earth. Abraham, man of faith, accepted the truth at that time. But what is that mystery? HE is GOD. HE shows Himself as an angel, human and at the same time HE is also Spirit. In His conversation with the Samaritan woman, JESUS called GOD the Father "Spirit" (John 4:24) GOD is Spirit. A real great secret is, if you could accept it, everything will be just fine. He is the WORD. He is the beginning and the end, the Alpha and the Omega.

Created: the best definition would be: To cause to come into existence. To produce. From the Hebrew word "bara": It means to create, to fashion. To make a thing which has not been made before. Another definition is: to bring into being, to make. And from the Greek word "ktizo" (pronounced "hktid-zo"), meaning to fabricate. These verbs in Greek denote, indicate or show the Almighty GOD in action, GOD conceiving the work of His Word, causing what is in His mind and Spirit to come to life and existence. The Word spoke it out and the Holy Spirit brings it into existence.

In the NOAB, the footnote said about verse 1: ..."what things were like when GOD started (e.g., when GOD began to create)".

The heavens: the expanse of space surrounding the earth, the sky, as far as our eyes or telescopes or satellites can go to see. The last time we check, that huge dome envelopes the whole universe. No wonder why King Solomon said "The heaven and heaven of heavens cannot contain Him...2 Chronicles 2:6". Pictures of scientists and astronomers show all the planets are into an infinite dome. Can we also say the offering? It is called the place of greater peace and beauty, the abode of GOD, the unexplainable awesome beauty, where most of us believe that angelic and celestial beings and spirits dwell. The place of the blessed, after life on earth... Wait a minute! Hold on! Most translations say "the heavens". It is plural then. Well, many other translations such as: "KJB, GWT, AKJV, DRB, ERV, WBT & ISV" say the "Universe" but, the some of the others like "NIV, NLT, ESV, NASB, HCSB, NET, ASV, DBT, WEB YLT" say "the heavens". How many heavens then? Well the apostle Paul in 2 Cor 12:2-4 said: "I know a man in Christ who fourteen (14) years ago -whether in the body I do not know, or out of the body I do not know' GOD knows- such a man was caught up to the third (3rd) heaven. And I know such a man -whether in the body or apart from the body I do not know, GOD knows- was caught up into Paradise and heard inexpressible words, which a man is not permitted to speak". (If there is a third, we are just saying..., there's a first, a second). Check also Deut 10:14, Eph 4:10, Heb 4:14.

It is also where GOD dwells with all the angelic beings. Does not GOD also dwell among us and in us? There are plenty of references in the Bible where many servants of the Lord have attempted to show where GOD dwells: Ps 2:4, 20:6, 2 Chron 2:6, 6:21, Job 22:12, Isa 57:15, Jer 23:24, Matt 10:32, 12:50, 18:10, Mark 11:25, Heb 8:1, Rev 8:1, Rev 21:22-27. The concept of GOD in us is mind blowing. Whether you want to believe it or not. This was not possible until Jesus Christ came. Because HE made it possible for the Lord GOD to dwell now in us (John17:21)

The heavens are also the huge dome that contains the galaxies, the stars and other planets. Isaiah 40:22 the prophet said that "the Lord stretches out the heavens like a curtain and spread them out like a tent to dwell in..." We then could agree with the concept of many heavens. And what about the all the planets may have been created or were already created and there was not any specific details about them in the Bible? The beginning talks about the heavens and the earth, not the heavens, the earth, and the other planets. This may not have anything to do with the beginning but, how in the world did the Magi decide to follow a star announcing the birth of a King?

And the earth: the planet on which we live. The earth is the 5th largest planet in the solar system. It is covered with water and land, but in the beginning was covered only with waters. It is also called the Globe because of its shape and roundness; but when God created it, it was formless and void Psalms 104:5-6 The author of this chapter is explaining the magnificence and the magnitude of the creation of GOD (You may read the whole chapter). He is also stated how the earth is being sustained on a foundation. Foundation? What foundation? Nothing is holding it up and down or from side to side, and especially when science can show pictures of the whole universe system. The sun, the moon and all the other planets stand on nothing. Talking about foundation? Some can say there is no GOD. That is fine. On our side, we believe there is a GOD, Creator of heavens and earth, Who reveal Himself in the person of JESUS.

God started to create things in an order...In going through the rest of the verses, if you pay great attention, you will see that verses 2-10 are the explanation of verse 1, a developmental detailed run down of verse 1; because verse 1 is not only a sentence in itself but also a summary of the creation of heaven and earth.

N.B.

In verse 6, GOD calls out a firmament (a great dome) to separate the waters.

the earth was a formless void and darkness covered the face of the deep...(NOAB)

The Zohar: In the goal of the creation said: Since there is no notion of time in the spiritual realm, we already exist in the ultimate perfect state in the world of infinity". Mmmhhhhh??? Is that strong and deep?

What was before the beginning then? The Word. GOD. The Word. John wrote about it, "In the beginning was the Word (John 1:1)". So, what was in the beginning? The Word. Now, look again, John 1:1 "In the beginning was the Word, and the Word was with GOD, and the Word was GOD". So, the Word was not alone, because the Word was with GOD, (Gen 1:26 "Let us make man..."). Who was in the beginning? The Word; and the Word was with GOD. GOD. In the beginning, GOD... In the very beginning probably goes deep into eternal times. Shall we dare asking: "Isn't it when God was about to create all things"? Before anything else? When GOD commences to execute into existence what is in his agenda, plan, mind.;, we need to consider that too. Gen 1:2 said: "...and the Spirit of God was moving over the surface of the waters". That's one of the reason why we must read some other versions of the Bible. The Apocrypha version (NOAB) the New Oxford Annotated Bible, which was recommended by the school where I studied said, "In the beginning when GOD created the heavens and the earth", meaning when GOD started bringing things to pass, bringing things forth, constructing or designing etc...

HE created the heavens first, and then the earth, HE started in an order; this is how it was, and verse 2 takes over by starting with the enumeration of things He's putting in place (Remember Job 38 and 39). Now we are going to open a big clause here. There was a book that I have read when I was in Haiti titled "La guerre de l'ame"; a word to word translation to English would be: *The war of the soul or The war for the soul"* to a certain extent. In this book, it is mentioned that a great war broke out in heaven; and Lucifer was kicked out with his followers (VERY IMPORTANT NOW. Read Jeremiah 4:19-28). Read also again verses 23-28. How was it then? Notice in these verses (GOD is talking through the prophet Jeremiah) that words like: heavens, no light, mountains and hills moved to and fro. And verse 25: "there was no man". So if there were no man, this means that if there were other beings, they were angelic beings, no man, no mankind. If there were other beings, who are they??? Let's continue now: Land, wilderness, cities..., Cities? And the end of verse 26... "the fierce anger of the Lord"? Now attach that part with verses 27 & 28. And continue to read from verses 29-31. That sounds like the gap theory but still, that argument doesn't stand.

Also consider: Revelation 12:7 "And there was war in heaven..." (NASB) And there was milchamah (war) in Shomayim... (OJB). How could there be war in heaven if something did not happen before or during the beginning? Now read chapter 12 again until verse 13. As we understand it, there is a lot in the beginning. If you could just read your Bible, GOD would show you HIMSELF and HIS plan. There is so much to say. Well the Bible paints out that everything has been done. everything is finished.

What about when Lucifer saw and thought he knew what GOD was about to do or, or, when he saw that what GOD had created was so beautiful, that envy and jealousy got into his heart. Remember the word of the Lord to Ezekiel, in Chapter 28:1-19. Does he know the law and principles of the Word? I bet he does. Notice: there is no mention in the beginning of angels, angelic beings until Gen 3:24; which also means that they were already there. One can easily conclude that they have been created before the heavens and earth, but it was not mention yet. What does that mean? When HE created the heavens (plural) that's probably when he also created the celestial beings or HE created them before that. How come in the angelic world there are angels, Cherubim, and Seraphim (Isaiah 6:2,6 the only place in the Bible where Seraphim is mentioned). Well, what do they look like? Matthew 28:2-3 described an angel. There's no picture. Believing before seeing. No wonder why in the spiritual realm it's believing first before seeing. Jesus called them blessed (John 20:29 "Blessed are those who have not seen and yet have come to believe"). There is blessing in believing beloved. <u>It also means that we need to read more, meditate more.</u> ***There's a process in everything***. Let GOD speak to us. So, if there is no mention of these particular beings in the beginning until the end of chapter 3, it also means that when GOD was busy doing something else or orchestrating the heavens; HE was busy creating a lot of other things such as the other planets, angelic beings at HIS service etc... and, who knows how much time is before verse

1 if there is and, how much time is between verse 1 and verse 2 if there is. What about the completeness of the heavens? There are so many assumptions to consider because, further down verse 2 said that the earth was without form and void or an empty waste...So there's no time in verses 1 and 2 (We're not in verse 2 yet) The story was reported to us this way. This is what we got. The Word of GOD is full with meaning (some even said; pregnant with meaning) like a lot of theologians, pastors, preachers said all the time. However this is just the way we see it and, the way we understand it. The creation of the world is complete in itself.

- *And the earth was tohu vavohu (without form, and void); and darkness was upon the face of the deep. And the Ruach Elohim was hovering upon the face of the waters (OJB)*
- *the earth was a formless void and darkness covered the face of the deep, while a wind from GOD swept over the face of the waters. (NOAB)*
- *The earth was formless and void, and darkness was over the surface of the deep, and the Spirit of GOD was moving over the surface of the waters. (NASB)*

Isaiah 45:18 "For thus said the Lord, who created the heavens (He is the GOD who form the earth and made it, He established it and did not create it a waste place, but formed it to be inhabited).(NASB)

Isaiah 45:18 "For thus says the Lord, He created the heavens (he is GOD!). These references are very critical and extremely important. You must stop, take a bible and look for them and read them. Now, these references are also ground for the gap theorists, especially this one, because of that part in the sentence that said (Isa 45:18...He established it and did not create it a waste place). They thought that GOD kicked out Lucifer and his rebellious angels to the earth, and because of that, it became void and an empty waste. Now If GOD kicked them while the earth was watery and a waste, that also means that they all went under water or GOD drowned them in the water, or in the abyss of the water. If GOD did this, why would the serpent be alive and be engaging into conversation with Eve. (We see even here there is choice in heaven, there is sin in heaven. It's not a bunch of robotic angels). But the verse is also states how it was when GOD created it, It was void; without contents. What about when the devil got into that conversation with GOD about Job? Why would the devil try to tempt the Lord after his baptism by John? Isn't the potter taking time to form his/her creation with a round ball of mud clay? While he/she is turning the potter's wheel in front of him/her, his/her mind is picturing in mind what he/she wants to do with it. Why the Spirit of GOD or a Whirlwind from GOD was hovering or moving over it? The Spirit of GOD is in motion over that ball of chaos. Look at the meaning of move or moving in the dictionary or in Google. Google it. I am hoping you can see this. The space around the earth was completely dark, according to the way the rest of the verse describes it. Can we say covered with darkness? The earth was mostly waters. Was there a first flood or destruction before the flood on Noah time? Was that the first flood; because the earth was just a mass of water, a big ball of water. Since the earth was formless and void, we wondered the reason why it went or was chaos. If we want to stay there, then we accept it was formless and void. We may come back to this. Or, like the Bible states it, that was the way GOD created it.

And the ***Spirit of GOD,*** a wind from GOD, another person in GOD, another person in the triune GOD. The vital character of GOD. Another part of GOD.. The essence of GOD. In Matthew 12:22-32 and Luke 12:10 where Jesus is telling the Pharisees and the Scribes about the unpardonable sin, which is blaspheming against the Holy Spirit. Why was that important? Why was it important for Him to stress on that important matter? One of the reasons is the holiness of GOD. He formed the earth and made it (he established it; he did not create it a chaos, he formed it to be inhabited!). (NOAB)

The first part of the sentence describes and explains itself. It was without form or shape, empty, but it was not like that. The gap theorists tried to score some points here. (***Isaiah 45:18; Jeremiah 4:23-28*** spells out the essential immaterial character of GOD. The Spirit of truth. Another strength from GOD. Some translations say a whirlwind from GOD, some say the Spirit of GOD, the NOAB said a wind from GOD swept over the face of the waters.

Well, consider this: Zechariah 14:9, Mark 12:29, John 10:30, 1 Corinthians 12:13, Ephesians 4:5. (Remember the word "paradox").

Now the followings should make you stop reading, go to your bible and check these verses: John 4:24 "GOD is spirit" JESUS said to the Samaritan woman;

- JESUS calls HIM the "Helper", some other versions say "the Comforter" and later on He calls Him "the Spirit of truth" who proceeds from the Father. Does not this reflect the love of GOD? (John 14:16); And in John 16:7 Jesus said "But I tell you the truth, it is to your advantage that I go away; for if I do not go away, the "helper" will not come to you; but if I go, I will send HIM to you. Wait a minute now. That's for free: if He will send the helper, He has some kind of authority, hasn't He. What authority does He have (John 15:26) to send the Spirit...? Him and the father are one, John 14:7,8-10; 18:11, etc... Mmhhh? ...I will send Him to you... Mmmhhh!!! That was free. Good GOD almighty!

- John 15:26 "When the Helper comes, whom I will send to you from the Father, that is the Spirit of truth who proceeds from the Father".

- And last but not the least; in John 16:13-15, "But when He, the Spirit of truth comes, He will guide you into all the truth, for He will not speak on his own initiative, but whatever He hears, He will speak; and He will disclose to you what is to come. He will glorify Me for He will take of Mine and will disclose it to you. All things that the Father has are Mine; therefore I said that He takes of Mine and will disclose it to you". What is that thing, that relationship between the Father, the Son and the Spirit? Yes, what's coming now is very heavy: John 16:12 "I have many more things to say to you, but you cannot bear them now" said JESUS to His disciples. GOD knows when one is ready. This is a very shrewd plan in the Triune GOD. The Spirit of GOD was about to get into major actions. JESUS will send

Him after He goes to the Father, to do what? To guide us, and instruct each of us who has a certain measure of balance, because the strength comes from submission, patience and endurance, to some of us gifts were and are given to speak in tongue, to interpret, to sing, to prophesy, to preach, to take care of people. Some don't understand, but He makes us understand; some have different gifts etc...but we are all in HIM.

Paradoxical? We can say so and sometimes we cannot say so, but that is really bold and strong.

And there are other things to consider. Remember, the first thing is to have the Bible to explain itself.

Well, since He is the essential essence of GOD, He was hovering, gliding and ready to set in action what the Word is about to pronounce over the face of the waters in front of Him. The Triune GOD: GOD, GOD the Spirit, GOD the Word, you also need to remember and consider that the Hebrew name for GOD is Elohim and it is plural.

A wind from GOD, a whirlwind from GOD. Verse 2 has a lot of theology into it.

࿔ Chapter 1, Verse 3-5 ࿔

Then GOD said, "Let there be light"; and there was light. And GOD saw that the light was good; and GOD separated the light from the darkness. GOD called the light Day, and the darkness He called Night. And there was evening and there was morning, the first day. (NOAB)

And Elohim said, Let there be light: and there was light [Tehillim 33:6,9] (And Elohim saw the light, that it was tov (good); and Elohim divided the ohr (light) from the choshech (darkness). And Elohim called the light Yom (Day), and the darkness He called Lailah (Night). And the erev (evening) and the boker (morning) were Yom Echad (Day One, the First Day, Mark 16:2). (OJB)

And GOD said, "Let there be light"; and there was light. And GOD saw the light, that it was good: and GOD divided the light from the darkness. And God called the light Day, and the darkness He called Night. And the evening and the morning were the first day. (KJV)

By the word of His mouth, God is saying... From verses 3 to 25, GOD is calling out the details of His creation, HE is speaking a lot of matters and things into existence, into being.

And the Word of GOD began orchestrating His power. Here we see the power is in the word; Because He said it and, it happens. He said: "Let there be... and there was". That is what is written. The footnote in the NASB version said: "Merely by speaking, GOD brought all thing into being". Psalms 33:6-9; "By the word of the Lord the heavens were made, and by the breath of his mouth all their host. He gathers the waters of the sea together as a heap; He lays up the deep in stores houses. Let all the earth fear the Lord; (these are the words of the Psalmist, not mine) Let all the inhabitants of the world stand in awe of Him. For He spoke, and it was done; He commanded, and it stood fast."

In other words, GOD pronounces His will and it is accomplished. GOD is decreeing what He has in mind and heart (We just dare saying that part). Shall I say what He was thinking, envisioning, imagining and it happened? He said it and it comes to pass. Let there be... and there was. In conclusion, this verse clearly demonstrates the almighty super power of GOD. The Lord's word will not return to Him void, but it shall accomplish that which He purpose (Isaiah 55:11), and succeed in the thing for which He sent it. If the Lord made very sure that His word does not return to Him void, how much more will He accomplish what He said about what is to come. What is "what is to come"? Matthew 24:4-9 and believers must get ready, because of what is to come. In these verses it is said: "See to it that no one misleads you. For many will come in My name, saying, 'I am the Christ', and will mislead many. You will be hearing of wars and rumors of wars. See that you are not frightened, for those things must take place, but that is not yet the end. For nation will rise against nation, and kingdom against kingdom, and in various places there will be famines and earthquakes. But all these things are merely the beginning of birth pangs. Then they will deliver you to tribulation, and will kill you, and you will be hated by all nations because of My name".

Now think about night without the stars and the moon and the day without the sun.

What is in all this for you reader? What is there for us to learn? 2 Corinthians 4:6 For GOD who said, "Light shall shine out of darkness," is the One who has shone in our hearts to give the Light of the knowledge of the glory of GOD in the face or Christ. This may be simple English but it is spiritual language. Moreover, the footnote in the NOAB is similar but in another tone: "The first of eight acts of creation through decree. Like a divine King GOD pronounces his will and it is accomplished." Psalms 97:4 said: "His lightnings lit up the world". And there's a word in 1Timothy 6:16 that gives to the light such a grandeur, by describing it with the word "inaccessible"; but most other versions said; "unapproachable"; though it is in that realm, it has become manifest, by dwelling among us. There are some other references that give more strength to this truth- for example, 2 Peter 1:19.

Do not confound: Let there be light in (v.4) with the sun which was created in (v.16) on the fourth day now.

John 8:12 Again Jesus spoke to them, saying, "I am the light of the world. Whoever follows me will never walk in darkness but will have the light of life." NOAB

When Jesus spoke to the people again, He said: "I am the light of the world; anyone who follows me will not be walking in the dark but will have the light of life." NJB

Remember what John 1:4 said: "in Him was life, and the life was the Light of men." Now, we enter another phase of orchestration; The goodness of creation. It is like action is becoming more tangible. Things start to come out in details, matters are coming out as the Lord GOD spoke. That's how the bible is describing it. Now GOD is affirming His Character, and meticulously entering into the detailing part of His creation. GOD has a plan for the completeness of the beauty of His creation and, it is about to be unfolded. After GOD saw that light was good, He then separated the light from the darkness, the Lord is sufficient and powerful. (Isaiah 45:7, I form the light and create darkness...); How did HE do that? How did HE separate light from darkness? Glad you have asked. As the Lord GOD is talking through his prophet Isaiah about Cyrus the Great (He is the liberator of the Jews who were captive in Babylonia. His name means "like the sun". He's the founder of the Persian empire (2 Chronicles 36:23) In that reference, GOD explains what His future creation will witness. In Isaiah 45:12: "I made the earth and created humankind upon it; it was my hands that stretched out the heavens, and I commanded all their hosts…" (notice the word "commanded"). The Lord ordained all the host of the heavens.

NB. Notice that GOD saw that the light **was good**. He divided the light from the darkness. Then, He gave them names…

Time is being separated, started and counted, with an evening and a morning. This is the first day.

Now, there is really no problem if someone thinks that it may have been a period of time; not because in 2 Peter 3:8 said: "But do not let this one fact escape your notice, beloved, that with the Lord one day is like a thousand years, and a thousand years like one day.

There are a few things to consider in that particular verse; the first day started at verse 3 when GOD start decreeing, calling things out, because in verse 1 and 2, there's no notion of time. In Genesis 2:1-6 where, in this account, the Bible comes with explanations of how GOD made things happens, How He created all things.

Another thing to consider also is the solar day of 24 hours. There was evening and there was morning. Genesis 1:14 God created lights in the dome to separate day and night also. Moses furthermore in (Exodus 20:11), reported the giving of the commandments of the Lord; where God started with an introduction of who He is, what He has done and the time of the creation of the world. Remember Moses talked to GOD face to face like a friend…Exodus 33:11. No wonder why researchers have attributed the authorship of the book of Genesis to Moses.

⮥ *Chapter 1, Verse 6* ⮤

And GOD said, "Let there be a dome in the midst of the waters, and let it separate the waters from the waters." (NOAB)

And Elohim said, Let there be a raki'a (expanse, dome, firmament) in the midst of the mayim (waters), and let it divide the mayim from the mayim. (OJB)

GOD made a vast huge expanse to separate waters from the waters. Waters all over the earth. Waters surround the earth??? Really? This is beautiful. Try to imagine how GOD is doing this. This is mind blowing. Try to read any bible with foot notes and see what they say about this. Try also to think about an artist in front of a canvas, who is making a live portrait of the nature in details on it.

1- Look at the definition of the word "expanse" in the dictionary. Let us write a couple of them for you: —an open or unbroken stretch; a wide, spreading surface.

Now, if the Pacific Ocean is a vast expanse of water, what about the sky above our heads? That dome that is much bigger than the earth alone. Remember the solar system. When you are in an airplane, and it's about to take of Waters above the earth, Job 26:8 said: "He fastens up the waters in his clouds, without the clouds giving way under their weight (NJB)." the NASB said: "He wraps up the waters in His clouds, and the cloud does not burst under them". And waters below on the earth, or waters over the surface of the earth... And the earth stands on nothing. Have you ever considered that? When you have a window seat in an airplane, and the airplane is passing through the thick clouds; when you go to the mountains and it's very foggy; have you ever thought about these creations of GOD? Look at the beauty that comes from the following 3 versions on the end of verse 7: "And hangs the earth upon nothing... And poised the earth on nothingness... And hangs the earth on nothing... (NOAB, NJB, NASB). I am sorry but I have to insert the french version here: "Il suspend la terre sur le neant". The french word "neant" here stands for: nothing, emptiness. Not a single thing or matter. Yes indeed, the earth stands on nothing, and when the Bible talks about Water within our reach (the ocean), water above our heads; according to the Dictionary, cloud means a visible mass of condensed water vapor floating in the atmosphere. Yes water in the form of clouds, suspended; separated by the dome. What is this? If He is not a powerful God. how can this be? And it is only after the first day. Whenever we are traveling on a flight, I stayed very amazed to contemplate the awesomeness of GOD. An upper one from a lower one (depending on where you are, that's how you should see it). If you try to think about the whole eight planets, how come they aren't held by anything in orbit? A gigantic dome surrounding the earth??? Not the earth alone now, because there are the other planets... Maybe GOD was busy doing or making or creating the other planets also. There are other pieces of information that we do not have.

The huge dome, or the expanse (Ps 19:1 David prophesied by saying in plural "the heavens are telling the glory of GOD"). Meanwhile you can try to picture at least the heaven and the earth in your mind, but in Revelation 20:11 "Then I saw a great white throne and Him who sat upon it, from whose presence earth and heaven fled away, and no place was found for them". People lift up their head and look in the sky and declare that this dome is heaven. And the Lord declares in Isaiah 66:1 "Thus said the Lord, heaven is My throne and the earth is My footstool." However, in Isaiah 65:17 It is said: "For behold, I create new heavens and a new earth" (NASB). So the Lord was talking through Isaiah the prophet about things to come. In the Expended Bible (EXB) it is written like this: "Look [Behold] I will make [create] new heavens and a new earth." and I will invite you in closing to read this portion of the book of Revelation 21:1-4 Amplified Bible, Classic Edition (AMPC)

1   Then I saw a new [a]sky (heaven) and a new earth, for the former [b]sky and the former earth had passed away (vanished), and there no longer existed any sea.

2   And I saw the holy city, the new Jerusalem, descending out of heaven from God, all arrayed like a bride beautified and adorned for her husband;

3   Then I heard a mighty voice from the throne and I perceived its distinct words, saying, See! The abode of God is with men, and He will live (encamp, tent) among them; and they shall be His people, and God shall personally be with them and be their God.

4   God will wipe away every tear from their eyes; and death shall be no more, neither shall there be anguish (sorrow and mourning) nor grief nor pain any more, for the old conditions and the former order of things have passed away.

༄ Chapter 1, Verse 7 ༄

And Elohim made the raki'a, and divided the waters under the raki'a from the waters which were above the raki'a; and it was so. (OJB)

So GOD made the dome and separated the waters that were under the dome from the waters that were above the dome. And It was so. (NOAB)

How did GOD do it? By His Word. By the power of His Word. The end of the verse said: "and it was so". So, what HE said came to be, or comes into existence.

Now, how can you separate water from water? Well, the Jewish people shared this event from generation to generation about their ancestors delivered from slavery in Egypt, when this GOD had them to cross over the red sea on dry ground (Exodus 14:10-22); did someone think about it for a moment? If this is not mind blowing for you. It's up to you. As for me, that's it. The Lord, not only did that miracle for his people through Moses, and the water, separating into two sides; nothing is holding them, and a huge path is created. There's no mud (but water was there for ages) Verse 16 said: "and the sons of Israel shall go through the midst of the sea on dry land." Check it out. Separate water from water? Really? But according to the way that people know water, how will they think about water being separated up and down, above and below. It seems like water is up, water is down. When you look at the sky, you can see huge chunks of clouds. What are these things? They got me into very deep thoughts when I am in a window seat on an airplane, contemplating pockets of small, medium, large, very big etc... of clouds, neither hanging on nothing, nor being held. Waters are being separated; not one recipient to another but from a place to another place. David described it as deep garment (good GOD Almighty) Psalms 104:6 "...the waters were standing above the mountains". What is that? Read verses 7,8 and 9.

1- Water in liquid form, running down from the mountains through the valley in to the great sea.
2- Water in vapor, in normal temperature, clouds; water in heat. Huge pouch of clouds which are a form of water, suspended in the air. Good GOD almighty! How come?

Water in liquid form that is very tangible. Water in vapor, clouds, huge pouch of clouds that can turn into liquid droplets to fall on earth... Who is this GOD??? HE even makes water float. Well, waters surround the earth... How can one separate waters from the waters by an expanse or a dome? Waters were like two walls in Exodus 14: 21,22 "...Then Moses stretched out his hand over the sea. The Lord drove the sea back by a strong east wind all night, and turned the sea into dry land; and the waters were divided. The Israelites went into the sea on dry ground, the waters forming a wall for them on their right and on their left". Here's another one: The Lord Jesus Christ, walking on water. What is that thing? Commanding the weather and the waters to be still, or rebuking the winds and the sea Matthew 8:26, Luke 8:25, Mark 4:39; and made Peter walked on water Matthew 14:29.

Isaiah 45:12 "It is I who made the earth, and created man upon it. I stretched out the heavens with My hands, and I ordained all their host". (NASB). Isaiah 48:13 etc... Why all these references? Well, they are there for us to check out and to believe.

Bad weather, and some part of the dome that covers with huge thick clouds, hung up on our heads are ready to come down causing heavy rain, flooding etc...

Chapter 1, Verse 8

And Elohim called the raki'a Shomayim (Heaven). And the erev and the boker were Yom Sheni (Day Two, the Second Day). (OJB)

GOD called the dome sky. And there was evening and there was morning, the second day. (NOAB)

GOD is continuing to give names to his creation. HE called the expense, the vault, the dome "heaven", some other translations say "sky". In some other versions, it can be translated by the word "Firmament", "dome", "expanse". This huge dome that we look at every day, when we lift up our heads to contemplate and to say: It's a beautiful day. We see a huge blue sky with a few bright white clouds and the sun. There's a big, big space that separates an upper ocean from a lower one. (Ps 148:4 Gen 7:11) Waters on the earth that GOD has created and, waters are suspended as clouds and vapor. That is all on the second day. In other words, verse 8 causes us to say that GOD created the heavens and the earth together. Vs 1. In the beginning, GOD created the heavens and the earth...

But isn't that dome goes beyond even the other planets? By asking that question, does not this ring a bell to see that it is not only the earth? Some among us think that the earth is the universe.

David described it as deep garment that covers or wraps around the whole earth (Psalms 104:6). There is absolutely nothing wrong with what he said. Why does David make such a statement?

What about the other planets? What about them? Are they in the Bible? It seems that the dome goes beyond planet earth.

And Elohim said, Let the waters under the heaven be gathered together unto one place, and let the yabashah (dry land) appear; and it was so. (OJB)

And GOD said, "Let the waters under the sky be gathered together into one place, and let the dry land appear." And it was so. (NOAB)

On the third day, yes on the third day, GOD made other major separations; gathering waters below the heavens into one place. I don't know what this speaks to you, but it is saying the order that GOD is setting all that He is saying or declaring into his creation. Remember it was a chaos (V2).

Was not the earth a ball of water or a mass of water? Or earth covered completely with water? Was the earth covered entirely with water? Was there a catastrophic judgment before that? Why would it be a mass of water? Verse 1, 2. Notice that GOD called dry land to appear. If there was a first judgment, it's like the earth and all the cities that it contained went all under the judgment of GOD. The Lord does not regret it. Well, Jeremiah was talking about the flood that happened in Noah's time or before Noah's time. Remember HE told Noah to take a pair of each kind of animals. Not all the animals entirely that were on the earth at that time.

Vs 1 again, GOD created the heavens and the earth. The earth. And verse 2 follows real quick like this: "the earth was a formless void.."(NOAB) and the (NASB) said; "the earth was formless and void..."

GOD said it and describe it Himself: "Let the waters under the sky be gathered together into one place..." And then come the creation of dry land. Yes, indeed. Dry land came out of the waters. Check also Job 38:18 "Have you comprehended the expanse of the earth?" When GOD was lecturing Job about the creation of the heavens and the earth.

❧ Chapter 1, Verse 10 ❧

And Elohim called the yabashah Eretz (Earth); and the mikveh (gathering together of the waters) called He Seas; and Elohim saw that it was tov. (OJB)

GOD called the dry land Earth, and the waters that were gathered together He called Seas. And GOD saw that it was good. (NOAB)

GOD called the dry land earth, and the gathering of the waters He called seas; and GOD saw that it was good. (NASB)

It was good. And it is good. Dry land. Solid ground with dirt. As GOD called her, she came out. Now remember that the word "Earth" is feminine. Keep this in mind. GOD called dry land to appear. Does it mean that the earth was in the water already??? Please don't ask me; but the word of GOD said that's what happened, so that is what it was. Well if so, we can assume a lot of hypotheses here. Since we lacksome other information, we can share what the footnote in the (NJB) New Jerusalem Bible at page 25: "There are several Babylonians stories of the flood which are in some respects remarkably similar to the biblical narrative." What about jumping to Jeremiah 4 again, from verses 23 t0 26. Read these 4 verses again and again. Does that insinuate a first flood? Well we cannot say that because does that mean that something happened before the beginning (Verse 26)? Take a look at www.genesisveracityfoundations.com. Waters are gathered together in verse 9. The waters of the globe, not water above.

Well, a very good question to ask is what was the shape or what was the form of the earth? Going back in verse two where it is said that the earth was formless and void. What exactly did it look like?

Now if we start reading Isaiah 24:1, 3-6, we can also go and read Revelation 21:1-2.

In short, creation is affected by the word of GOD.

❧ Chapter 1, Verse 11-13 ❧

And Elohim said, Let the earth bring forth vegetation, the herb yielding zera (seed), and the fruit tree yielding pri (fruit) after its kind, whose seed is in itself, upon the earth; and it was so. And the earth brought forth vegetation, and herb yielding zera (seed) after its kind, and the tree yielding fruit, whose seed was in itself, after its kind; and Elohim saw that it was tov(good). And the erev and the boker were Yom Shlishi (Day three, the third day). (OJB)

Then GOD said, "Let the earth put forth vegetation: plants yielding seed, and fruit trees of every kind on earth that bear fruit with seed in it." And it was so. The earth brought forth vegetation: plants yielding seed of every kind, and trees of every kind bearing fruit with the seed in it. And GOD saw that it was good. And there was evening and there was morning, the third day. (NOAB)

We are now on the third day.

GOD called the earth to bring out vegetation, grass, herb, and fruit. This is happening upon showing the earth obeying the word of GOD. (Luke 8:25) The earth yields to what GOD said. And also, now read Genesis 2:4-9. This portion explains how it all happened. We are on the third day. GOD is expressing His creative work. The foot note in the Apocrypha Bible has brought an interesting comment. It says that the word "earth in Hebrew is feminine. If it is feminine, then it also means a lot of other things. In some other languages around the world, there's a great distinction in the family of words or nouns. Like the word "earth" is feminine in Hebrew, it is also feminine in French. Take a deep breath. Picture it. GOD is having the earth now to become fertile, productive, Psalm 65:9-10 "You visit the earth and cause it to overflow; you greatly enrich it; The stream of GOD is full of water; you prepare the grain, for thus you prepare the earth. You water its furrows abundantly, you settle its ridges, you soften it with flowers, you bless its growth. Genesis 41:47 "During the seven years of plenty the land brought forth abundantly".

For GOD to put out such a command, and the earth to yield to that command, speaks of the earth having ears to listen and obey to that command. This also means that the earth was complete in herself when GOD made it; because further down in that same chapter 2, the earth is yielding vegetation of all kinds and man will be coming out of her also.

Onn the third day GOD is done with trees, vegetation, fruits, in other words HE prepares real natural food for HIS future creation which going to be animals and mankind.

ᖇ Chapter 1, Verses 14-19 (Why this big jump of 6 verses?) ᖆ

14- And Elohim said, Let there be lights in the raki'a of the heaven to divide the day from the night; and let them be for otot (signs), and for mo'adim (seasons), and for yamim (days), and shanim (years); 15 And let them be for lights in the raki'a of the heaven to give light upon the earth; and it was so. 16 And Elohim made two great lights; the greater light to rule the day, and the lesser light to rule the night; He made the kokhavim (stars) also. 17 And Elohim set them in the raki'a of the heaven to give light upon the earth, 18 And to rule over the day and over the night, and to divide the light from the darkness; and Elohim saw that it was tov. 19 And the erev and the boker were Yom Revi'i (Day Four, the Fourth Day).

14- And GOD said, "Let there be lights in the dome of the sky to separate the day from the night; and let them be for signs and for seasons and for days and years, And it was so. 15- and let them be lights in the dome of the sky to give light upon the earth." 16- GOD made the two great lights—the greater light to rule the day and the lesser light to rule the night— and the stars. 17- GOD set them in the dome of the skyto give light upon the earth, 18- to rule over the day and over the night, and to separate the light from the darkness. And GOD saw that it was good. And there was evening there was morning, the fourth day. (NOAB)

Lights: Plural, to separate day from the night. GOD gave details of what HE was about to create, or what HE is separating. HE explains continuously how and what they will be. The moon and the sun plus the stars. Remember the day starts at night.

The NJB said "Let there be light in the vault of heaven to divide day from night..." The great sun.

❧ Chapter 1, Verses 20, 21, 22, 23 ❦

20- And Elohim said, Let the waters bring forth an abundance of living creatures, and fowl that may fly above the earth in the open raki'a of heaven. 21 And Elohim created great sea creatures, and every living creature that moveth, which the waters brought forth in abundance, after their kind, and every winged fowl after its kind; and Elohim saw that it was tov. 22 And Elohim blessed them, saying, Be fruitful, and multiply, and fill the waters in the seas, and let fowl multiply in the earth. 23 And the erev and the boker were Yom Chamishi (Day Five, the Fifth Day). (OJB)

20- And GOD said, "Let the waters bring forth swarms of living creatures, and let birds fly above the earth across the dome of the sky."

So GOD created the great sea monsters and every living creature that moves, of every kind, with which the waters swarm, and every winged bird of every kind. And GOD saw that it was good. GOD blessed them, saying, "Be fruitful and multiply and fill the waters in the seas, and let birds multiply on the earth."

And there was evening and there was morning, the fifth day. (NOAB)

Here's another jump of 4 verses. How does GOD do it? Merely by commanding them to happen. Look at what happens in the very beginning. Indeed, how did GOD do it? Whatever is in HIS mind, HE called it out. GOD did this for the waters and on the next verse, HE will do it for the land too.

Moving creatures now are coming on the scene, creatures that have life; whether it was in water or on land. GOD blessed them. These are the key words. Yes indeed, GOD blessed them and talked to them, told them what to do. To do what? HE told them to be fruitful and multiply and fill the waters in the seas and the fowl to do the same in the earth. (Verse 22, GOD talked to the sea creatures.) And the sea creatures listened and obeyed.

Now during the flood in time of Noah, the Lord ordered Noah to take two kinds of each animal (Gen 6: 19,20), male and female, but HE did not say that for the creatures in the water. Common sense now; HE did not order Noah to do the same for the creatures in the water. Do you see that?

❧ Chapter 1, Verses 24, 25 ❧

24- And G-d said, Let the earth bring forth the living creature after its kind, cattle, and creeping thing, and beast of the earth after its kind; and it was so.

25 And G-d made the beast of the earth after its kind, and cattle after their kind, and every thing that creepeth upon the earth after its kind; and G-d saw that it was tov. (OJB)

24- And GOD said, "let the earth bring forth living creatures of every kind: cattle and creeping things and wild animals of the earth of every kind". And it was so. GOD made the wild animals of the earth of every kind, and the cattle of every kind, and everything that creeps upon the ground of every kind. And GOD saw that it was good. (NOAB)

As GOD did with filling the waters with sea animals and living creatures, so HE did for the earth with animals and creeping things. GOD brought forth life in all creatures HE created. Even (remember verse 12), plants have life into themselves. GOD called them out again.

From the earth now HE called the terrestrial animals. Remember verse 11, where HE called the earth to bring forth vegetation. The earth did so at verse 12. Read them again.

Genesis 6:19-20

✑ Chapter 1, Verses 26, 27 ✑

26- And G-d said, Let Us make man in Our tzelem, after Our demut: and let them have dominion over the fish of the sea, and over the fowl of the air, and over the cattle, and over all the earth, and over every creeping thing that creepeth upon ha'aretz (the earth). 27- So G-d created humankind in His own tzelem, in the tzelem Elohim (image of G-d) created He him; zachar (male) and nekevah (female) created He them. (OJB)

26- Then GOD said, "Let Us make humankind in our image, according to our likeness; and let them have dominion over the fish of the sea, and over the birds of the air, and over the cattle, and over the cattle, and over all the wild animals of the earth, and over over every creeping thing that creeps upon the earth." 27- So GOD created humankind in His image, in the image of GOD HE created them; male and female HE created them. (NOAB)

Now we go deeper into a very interesting point. The Triune GOD is about to make a replica of HIMSELF or THEMSELVES. (Is that paradoxical? Don't ask me. You've got to find out for yourself). Yes! GOD is about to make other gods like HIM, whom will be like HIM in all righteousness and holiness. It means that the whole godhead was not in action since the first day. Many people believe that GOD is only a single person. NO, no, no, no, no! Remember that the word (Elohim) is plural in Hebrew. Open your mind now brothers and sisters: *John 15:26 "When the Helper comes, whom **I** will send to you from the Father, that is the Spirit of truth who proceeds from the Ftaher, Hwill testify about Me."; John 16:7 "But I tell you the truth, it is to your advantage that I go away; for if I do not go away, the Helper will not come to you; but if I go, **I** will send Him to you." John 16:13-15 "But when He, the Spirit of truth comes, He will guide you into all the truth, for He will not speak on His own Initiative, but whatever He hears, He will speak, and He will disclose to you what is to come. 14 He will glorify Me, for He will take of Mine and will disclose it to you. 15 All things that the Father has are mine; therefore I said that He takes of Mine and will disclose it to you. John 17:20,21 I do not ask on behalf of these alone, but for those also who believe in Me through their word; 21 that they may all be one; even as you, Father, are in Me and **I** in You, that they also may be in **Us**, so that the world may believe that you sent Me. And to conclude this phase, let us close this part with John 17:22 "The glory which You have given Me I have given to them, that they may be one, just as We are one."*

What about the fact that humankind IS ABOUT to be in the image of GOD, in His own characteristics? What's in the mind of GOD when HE is about to create man like them (like the Father, Son, Spirit)? The footnote in the NOAB version said: *"The plural us, our (Genesis 3:22;*

11:7) probably refers to the divine beings who compose GOD's heavenly court (1 Kings 22:19)(Is 6:8)". Another footnote in the NASB version said "image...likeness. No distinction should be made between "image" and "likeness," which are synonyms in both the OT (Gen 5:1, Gen 9:6) and the NT (1Cor11:7; Col 3:10; James 3:9). Since man is made in GOD's image, every human being is worthy of honor and respect; he is neither to be murdered (Gen 9:6) nor cursed (James 3:9).

Man is made in GOD's image. In HIS likeness John 10:34, "Jesus answered, Is it not written in your law, I said, you are gods"? Since they are believers in GOD, Jesus was calling them back to the Scriptures that they know so well, (Psalms 82:6). If you are paying close attention to your reading, read that particular verse again. Have you noticed: "I said"? If GOD is about to make man in HIS image and resemblance, one can just tell that authority is coming after. GOD has a specific plan.

Well, was it a kind of cloning? Duplication? Well, does duplication sounds better? Duplication is like replicating but at another level. What was in the mind of GOD when HE made that decision, when HE took that action? Do you really want to know? Well, we don't know. Only GOD knows HIS mind. KJV version plus my paraphrases in parentheses "Let us make man in our image (according to what we resemble), after our likeness (looking just exactly like us): and let them have dominion over... (let's give them power).

Wait a minute now. Adam and Eve are in training already (verse 27) (that's what I call it). A process has begun because, when GOD brought all the animals including the birds to him to see what he would call them (Gen 2:19); from right there one can see the likeness of man with GOD. That's a great beginning. What's happening in the spirit? Something is happening in the spirit. What is it? Don't ask me. Remember we have to read, search, study and meditate. If something else were not happening in the spirit world of GOD and Adam, how would he know what to name the animals? Why would GOD bring the animals to him to name? Now we are going to drop the verses that came to our spirit when we were writing this segment: John 15:1-11 and verses 1-4 alone should tell you something; John 16:26,27; There is a cause in there. verse 27 shows it because it shows the Father as a caring father, teaching and guiding His likeness. There is so much to say here. Well, we will come back to these verses. Meanwhile, try to picture Adam and Eve walking in the garden and GOD as a Spirit is with them or GOD, is walking along side of them, unseen, invisible, in them. WOW! Wait a minute! Wow!!! Can I say that? Please refer to Book 2 to further expound on this subject.

In our Image and Likeness. According to our image and resemblance. Let us make man like us. Jesus said to the Samaritan woman: "<u>GOD is Spirit</u>"; since GOD is spirit, therefore HE created us spirits like HIM. The power of GOD has a lot to do with the scriptures. GOD has documented everything. If HE said: "Let us make... like us...? Can we try to conceive this in our mind. Are they or are they not in the visible or invisible at that time, then what did GOD make? What did HE create? Or what type of body did HE make them with? Is it a body that can float in the air, transparent or transcendent that can be visible and invisible? No one can see GOD or as it is written in Exodus 33:20 "...for no man can see Me and live". Indeed, it's not the same context; but I want you to understand something. I am just reminding you what is written. A spirit is not bound by anything. The spirit of GOD was hovering, sweeping over, moved upon, moving over, hovering the surface of the waters. A spirit can go through anything. Was there a body? Were there bodies? That answer will be in chapter 2. But, after the resurrection of the Lord Jesus-Christ, The Son of the living GOD, when HE appeared to the disciples after vanishing from their sight (Luke 24:31), and in Luke 24:36-49, Jesus came out of nowhere. He just came and stood in their midst; especially verse 39: "See my hands and my feet, that is I Myself; touch me and see, for a spirit does not have flesh and bones as you see that I have." Then HE asked them for something to eat in verse 41. A Spirit or a ghost? Vanishing? (Luke 24:31) Disappearing? The disciples could not believe it (V 32). But let's consider this: He asked them for something to eat because they are all quiet, frightened, astounded, some of them were there when He was beaten and killed. They knew what happened. They witnessed the Son of GOD, the Son of man tortured, mutilated, executed, pierced on the side by a Roman soldier to make sure He is dead. He died and was carried to the tomb where the dead reside. John his brother was probably there comforting his mother; but let me tell you there was one thing not in the ordinary with this dead man. There was one thing extraordinary with this dead man. Now HE's in their midst? How can that be? How can this be possible? This is becoming supernatural. They forgot what HE said to them, they are thinking ghost, zombies, zombie apocalypse... Would not you feel the same way? Maybe some of them wanted to get up and run. HE asked them for something to eat and they gave something to Him to eat. HE disappeared. HE vanished. What about the food HE just ate? Mmmhhhhh??? I will let you think. Read and reflect also on John chapter 21.

But after the resurrection, GOD has fixed us the way HE wanted us to be (HE did it in Gen 3:21). That is exactly what JESUS-CHRIST has accomplished. Humble ourselves to Him. Live a godly life and HE restores us to our original state. Paradoxical. Isn't it? In the twinkling of an eye...(1Cor15:51-53) Mystery... We will be changed... Imperishable... Incorruptible...Getting back to immortality. Hallelujah! Praise be to our GOD! By just believing, trusting in the Lord. Like Thomas said: "My Lord and my GOD!" (John 20:28). But read John 20:19-29 again and again. You will see a lot of transcendence in there. Notice his unbelieving attitude (vs 24,25) Jesus came in their midst (Vs 26,27) to take away Thomas' doubt, and yes, HE made Thomas touch HIM (Meanwhile JESUS is incorruptible now with this holistic body) The doors were shut (v 26), HE didn't knock; no one went to open the doors. Can you see this? We also belong to the spiritual world.

Going back to verse 24, GOD was creating from the earth now. From the earth GOD created living creatures, cattle, creeping things and wild animals or beasts. This is day (6) six. Creation took another turn. GOD stopped commanding, declaring and calling things out. Now it looks likes that HE is about get someone else involved or some others involved, if we may say so into what HE is about to do. HE called someone else into consultation (John 1:1-3; *In the beginning was the Word, and the Word was with GOD, and the Word was GOD. He was in the beginning with GOD). All things came into being through Him, and apart from Him nothing came into being that has come into being."* Does that mean that this person was not there when HE was doing all that? No. This person was there *(John 17:5 "So now, Father, glorify me in your own presence with the glory that I had in your presence before the world existed")*. Also please read Proverbs chapter 8 (very important). HE continued and said (GOD in Him, Him in GOD) The Spirit is hovering too right there: "Let us make humankind in our image". Adam a Hebrew word for man, human being, and according to GOD, according to us, according to what we look like, like we are; the idea was (is) to make a spirit like them (Us) into what they resemble and let's give him a form like us. Male and female like us? Male and female like us, HE created them, according to that famous verse of 27. He created both of them. "In the image of GOD created he him..." Adam has Eve within himself. (in chapter 2:21,22) GOD gets Adam to sleep, to form Eve with one of his ribs). HE created them as a spirit like HIM, male and female, (GOD is spirit...) Is the spirit of GOD visible? Ezekiel 1:12...??? Eve also knew what the instructions or commandments of GOD were. Since GOD said: "Let us make them like us", HE immediately gave them power and dominion over some of the things we created.

So... THEY, (US) created man in the image of GOD HE created him, male and female. Okay Now, man is male and female. GOD is male and female. GOD made a spiritual man and a spiritual woman. GOD is him and her and GOD, is spirit.

GOD called Someone else who was with Him, who was with Him before the world begins, to replicate another "Them, or Us". GOD made divine being like HIM. Male and female. It also seems that at the moment made them, basic knowledge and instructions were already instilled in them because, once HE created them (End of verse 27) HE blessed them (vs 28) HE starts giving them instructions

(Be fruitful, multiply, and fill the earth and...) plus dominion, (subdue it and rule...)

Son of GOD, spiritually, stepped foot on the earth by becoming flesh to rebuke the lie that our ancestor believed. Son of man, to pay the wrath of GOD in HIS fierce anger against sin. Who could accuse HIM of sin? John 8:46 said "Which one of you convicts Me of sin..."? This is a very powerful sentence.

We are spiritual beings, because we come from GOD. He created us like HIM. Let this sink in you.

❧ *Chapter 1, Verse 28* ❧

And G-d blessed them, and G-d said unto them, Be fruitful, and multiply, and fill the earth, and subdue it: and have dominion over the fish of the sea, and over the fowl of the air, and over every living thing that moveth upon the earth. (OJB)

GOD bless them, and GOD said to them, "Be fruitful and multiply, and fill the earth and subdue it; and have dominion over the fish of the sea and over the birds of the air and over every living thing that moves upon the earth." (NOAB),

The day before, the fifth day (Vs 20-23). GOD created swarms of living creatures from the waters and birds of the sky, living creatures that move and **blessed** them and ordered them to multiply, fill the earth and the waters.

But to the humankind -besides the mandate to multiply and fill the earth- HE said one more thing: "Subdue it" (Vs 28) This means to make subservient, dominate, bring under control. The Hebrew word is "***kabash***" in Hebrew (bring into subjection).

GOD blessed them, pronounces good tidings over them, invokes divine favor upon them. He empowered them over the earth. He told them to do five (5) things:

1- To be fruitful
2- To multiply
3- To fill the earth
4- To subdue it
5- To rule

But to the animal kingdom He told them the first two: "Be fruitful and multiply and fill"(Gen 1:22)

After the flood in Genesis chapter 8, When GOD remember Noah and his family, and that the water subsided, Noah built an altar to the Lord, and offered burnt offerings (v 20), but in Gen 9:1 GOD is giving the same instructions to Noah: "Be fruitful and multiply and fill the earth". The difference here is that GOD has said to Adam and Eve to subdue and also to rule, but did not say that to Noah and family; and from verses 2 to 7, HE started with the "fear" and "terror". What does that mean?

Faith is coming out. Words of blessings and power. GOD gives his likeness and resemblance powers, not all powers like HE gave to His Son. But how are they going to process these powers? Well, it seems they were doing good until Genesis 2:25. Things were really great and going excellent. They were naked and were not ashamed. Some of you may, well it is the two of them only anyway. Why should they be ashamed? From there, you also have to look at purity and holiness. They are like GOD.

Chapter 1, Verse 29

And G-d said, Hinei, I have given you every herb bearing seed, which is upon the face of kol ha'aretz (all the earth), and every etz (tree), in the which is the fruit of a tree yielding seed; to you it shall be for food.(OJB)

GOD said, "See, I have given you every plant yielding seed that is upon the face of all the earth, and every tree with seed in its fruit; you shall have them for food. OAB)

Now GOD the provider is into action again. HE proceeded with provision of food, food to sustain Adam. He is not a robot; and it seems That the LORD gave him a vegetarian diet. It is literally a vegetarian diet. Well indeed, the verse is very plain. There's no loopholes. Notice also that all animals are herbivores. Plant yielding seed, and every tree which has fruit yielding seed. Now, how would Adam and Eve know all this if GOD did not inculcate some knowledge in them? It may be hard to conceive for some, but remember "GOD is Spirit". He created them like Him. Mmhhhhhh??? In the book of Psalm at chapter 104, verse 27; it is written: "... to give them their food in due season." And the foot note in the NASB version said: "By GOD's benevolent care this zoological garden flourishes.

❧ Chapter 1, Verse 30 ❧

And to every beast of the earth, and to every fowl of the air, and to every thing that creepeth upon the earth, wherein there is life, I have given every green herb for food; and it was so. (OJB)

And to every beast of the earth and to every bird of the air, and to everything that creeps on the earth, everything that has the breath of life, I have given every green plant for food". And it was so. NOAB

Psalms 145:15-16

Job 38:41

In both the beast of the earth and the fowl of the air, God has created a living soul.

GOD made complete provision for the animal kingdom. All animals have a vegetarian diet. All animals at that particular time are herbivores. No animals preying on other animals or no animals eating other animals, even in the sea. That will change later in the future. Why and how? That will be in the third book in Genesis 3. After the flood in Genesis chapter 8, When GOD remember Noah and his family, and that the water subsided. Noah built an alter to the Lord, and offered burnt offerings (v 20), but in Gen 9:1 GOD is giving the same instructions to Noah: "Be fruitful and multiply and fill the earth". Well, Adam and Eve had their instructions. It's like HE also told them not to worry about the animal kingdom. Don't worry about them. They got it. Follow what you have been told. That's the way we understand it.

Genesis 9:3 said: "Every moving thing that is alive shall be food for you; I give all to you, and as I gave the green plant." The study according to the foot note of the NASB version

❧ *Chapter 1, Verse 31* ❧

And G-d saw that everything that He had made, and, behold it was tov me'od (very good). And the erev and the boker were Yom Shishi (day six, the Sixth Day). (OJB)

GOD saw that everything that He had made, and indeed, It was very good. And there was evening and there was morning, the sixth day. (NOAB)

Psalms 104:24

O Lord, how manifold are your works! In wisdom you have made them all; the earth is full of your creatures.

1 Timothy 4:4

For every creature of God is good, and nothing to be refused, if it be received with thanksgiving;

"And so it was.", according to the New Jerusalem Bible. Indeed, GOD has finished working for six days. How many hours did HE work a day? Don't ask me. Let's go do some research on it.

HE contemplates, reviews HIS works, everything was indeed perfect and very good. At each creation, GOD saw the manifestation to be good. GOD did not make any mistakes. Who are we to say anything about this great creation. Everything is all around us every day. We cannot even create anything that HE did not create already. If ever we invent something, it's all taken out of the creation of GOD. Well, GOD is very satisfied of all that HE had made, because everything that GOD had created was not just good, but very good. GOD is good and does good... (Psalms 119:68). Everything went exactly the way HE intended things to be. Everything and their hosts were completely accomplished. Nothing was missing. GOD is now ready to get some rest.

TO YOU ALONE OH GOD, BE ALL THE GLORY! FOREVER AND EVER! AND EVER AND EVER. AMEN!

WHY THIS WHOLE PLAIDOIRIE (French for expository speech or defense speech)? But who am I to defend the Word of God, which is the ultimate truth?

Malachi 3:1 Behold, I will send my messenger, and he shall prepare the way before ME: and the Lord, whom ye seek, shall suddenly come to his temple, even the messenger of the covenant, whom ye delight in: behold, He shall come sayeth the Lord of hosts.

Repent! Repent! For the kingdom of heaven is at hand. We are not repenting to escape eternal death, but we are doing so, because the Word of GOD is true. The Word of GOD is JESUS, The Christ; the Son of the living GOD. HE is the only Truth.

Acts 17:30-31 "While GOD has overlooked the times of human ignorance, now HE commands all people everywhere to repent, because HE has fixed a day on which HE will have the world judged in righteousness by a man whom HE has appointed, and of this HE has given assurance to all by raising Him from the dead".

The Bible declares in Hebrews 3:7 "Therefore, just as the Holy Spirit says, TODAY IF YOU HEAR HIS VOICE, DO NOT HARDEN YOUR HEARTS... Psalms 95:7,

Luke 5:32 "I have not come to call the righteous but sinners to repentance".

Matthew 11:28 "Come to me all who are weary and heavy laden, and I will give you rest".

Matthew 11:27 "All things have been handed over to me by my Father; and no one knows the Son except the Father; nor does anyone know the Father except the Son..."

John 14:6 "I am the way, and the truth, and the life; No one comes to the Father but through Me".

Acts 17:30-31 "While GOD has overlooked the times of human ignorance, now HE commands all people everywhere to repent, because HE has fixed a day on which HE will have the world judged in righteousness by a man whom HE has appointed, and of this HE has given assurance to all by raising Him from the dead".

Hebrews 4:13 "And there is no creature hidden from His sight, but all things are open and laid bare to the eyes of Him with whom we have to do".

Hebrews 3:7-8 Therefore, just as the Holy Spirit says, "Today if you hear His voice, do not harden your hearts...

Hebrews 4:11-16 "Therefore let us be diligent to enter that rest, so that no one will fall, through following the same example of disobedience.

For the word of GOD is living and active and sharper than any two-edged sword and piercing as far as the division of soul and spirit, of both joints and marrow, and able to judge the thoughts and intentions of the heart.

And there is no creature hidden from His sight, but all things are open and laid bare to the eyes of Him with whom we have to do.

Therefore, since we have a great high priest who has passed through the heavens, JESUS the Son of GOD, let us hold fast our confession.

For we do not have a high priest who cannot sympathize with our weaknesses, but One who has been tempting in all things as we are, yet without sin.

Therefore, let us draw near with confidence to the throne of grace, so that we may receive mercy and find grace to help in time of need".

<u>GOD alone is good. There's none like HIM. To HIM alone be glory forever and ever. Amen, amen, and amen.</u>

Born on February 5th, 1963 in Port-au-Prince, Haïti. Migrated in the USA on November 1995. He's been living in Atlanta, GA with his son. He is an avid lover of the Word, who is always telling people to read their Bible. He has a certificate degree from (ITC) Interdenominational Theological Center, a very well known school of Theology. He is a freelance preacher and author.

Lightning Source UK Ltd.
Milton Keynes UK
UKHW011825250219
337978UK00001B/8/P